English Grammar for Students of German

The Study Guide for Those Learning German

Third edition WITHDRAWN

Cecile Zorach
Charlotte Melin

The Olivia and Hill Press®

English Grammar series
edited by Jacqueline Morton

English Grammar for Students of French
English Grammar for Students of Spanish
English Grammar for Students of Italian
English Grammar for Students of Latin
English Grammar for Students of Russian
English Grammar for Students of Japanese

Gramática española para estudiantes de inglés

© 1994, Jacqueline Morton

Printed in the U.S.A.

ISBN 0-934034-23-0

CONTENTS

To the Student   vii

Introduction   1

1. What is a Noun?   4

2. What is Meant by Gender?   6

3. What is Meant by Number?   9

4. What are Articles?   11
   Definite Articles   11
   Indefinite Articles   12

5. What is Meant by Case?   15
   Case of English Pronouns   15
   Case of German Nouns   18

6. What is a Verb?   21
   Transitive and Intransitive Verbs   22

7. What is a Subject?   24

8. What are Objects?   26
   Direct Object   26
   Indirect Object   28
   Sentences with a Direct and an Indirect Object   29
   Object of a Preposition   29

9. What is a Predicate Noun?   32

10. What is the Possessive?   34

11. What is a Pronoun?   38

12. What is a Personal Pronoun?   40
    Personal Pronouns as Subjects   40
    Personal Pronouns as Objects   43
    Personal Pronouns as Objects of Prepositions   48

13. What are the Principal Parts of a Verb?   52

14. What is an Infinitive?   55

15. What is a Verb Conjugation?   57
    Verb Subjects   57
    Verb Forms   60

16. What is Meant by Tense?   62

17. What is the Present Tense?   63

18. What is the Past Tense?   65
19. What are Auxiliary Verbs?   67
    Use of Auxiliaries in English and German   68
    Modal Auxiliaries   69
20. What is a Participle?   71
    Present Participle   71
    Present Participle Versus Gerund   73
    Past Participle   75
21. What are the Perfect Tenses?   79
22. What is the Future Tense?   83
23. What is Meant by Mood?   86
24. What is the Imperative?   88
25. What is the Subjunctive?   90
    The General Subjunctive (Subjunctive II)   92
    The **würde**-Construction   95
26. What is Meant by Direct and Indirect Discourse?   97
27. What is a Possessive Pronoun?   100
28. What is a Reflexive Pronoun?   102
29. What is a Reflexive Verb?   106
30. What is an Interrogative Pronoun?   108
    Persons   110
        1. Subject: **Wer**?   110
        2. Object: **Wen**? or **Wem**?   110
        3. Indirect Object: **Wem**?   111
        4. Object of a Preposition: **Wen**? or **Wem**?   111
        5. Possessive: **Wessen**?   112
    Things: **Was**?   112
31. What is a Relative Pronoun?   114
    Use of Relative Pronouns   119
    Relative Clauses with Indefinite Antecedents   120
    Restrictive Clauses Versus Non-Restrictive Clauses   121
32. What is an Adjective?   123
33. What is a Descriptive Adjective?   124
34. What is Meant by Comparison of Adjectives?   128
    Comparative   128
    Superlative   130

35. What is a Possessive Adjective?   133
36. What is an Interrogative Adjective?   136
37. What is an Adverb?   139
38. What is a Preposition?   141
    Two-Way Prepositions   142
    Preposition or Prefix?   144
39. What are Prefixes and Suffixes?   146
    Nouns Forms with Suffixes   147
    Verbs Formed with Prefixes   147
40. What is Meant by Active and Passive Voice?   150
41. What is a Conjunction?   156
    Preposition or Subordinating Conjunction?   156
42. What are Sentences, Phrases, and Clauses?   159
    What is a Sentence?   159
    What is a Phrase?   160
    What is a Clause?   161
    Simple Sentences   161
    Compound Sentences   162
    Complex Sentences   163
Appendix—Selected Noun Gender Reference List   167
Answer Key   169
Index   173

To the Student

English Grammar for Students of German explains the grammatical terms that are in your German textbook and shows you how they relate to English grammar. The explanations and numerous examples in this handbook compare English and German grammar and point out some of the similarities and differences between the two languages. Once you understand the terms and concepts in your own language, it will be easier for you to learn how they apply to German.

Before you do your German homework, pick out the grammatical terms and concepts covered in the lesson you are about to study. Then, consult the index of *English Grammar for Students of German* to see where these topics are covered. Read the relevant pages carefully, making sure that you understand the explanations and examples. Finally, do the **Review** at the end of the chapters you have read and compare your answers with the ones in the **Answer Key** at the end of the handbook.

Tips for Studying a Foreign Language

1. RULES—Make sure you understand each rule before you move on to the next one. Language learning is like building a house, each brick is only as secure as its foundation.

2. MEMORIZATION—Memorization plays an important part in language learning. You will have to memorize vocabulary, verb conjugations, grammar rules, etc. Here are some steps to follow when you memorize new material:

   - Divide the passage into sections you can easily remember (for instance, 2 sentences or 5 words).

   - Read the section aloud several times.

   - Write the words down as you repeat them aloud to yourself.

   - Compare what you have written with the original.

   - Repeat the steps above until you can write what you have learned without mistakes.

   - Go on to memorize the next section in the same way.

   - Work at memorizing for only short periods of time. If you find you are not concentrating on the material, take a break or do a different part of your assignment.

3. **Vocabulary**—Use any trick or gimmick that will help you remember German words. Here are some that students have found useful.

   - Write each word on a different index card: German on one side, English on the other.

   - Use index cards of different colors to help you remember useful information: the gender of nouns (i.e., blue for masculine, red for feminine, yellow for neuter), or the parts of speech (i.e., green for verbs, orange for adjectives, etc.).

   - When learning the words, flip through the cards looking at the German word. Say the word aloud, then think of the English word that corresponds. Flip the card to check your answer. Shuffle the deck often so that words do not always appear in the same order. As you learn words, place those cards in a separate pile and concentrate on the ones you still need to learn.

   - As you memorize, organize the cards in different groupings and spread them out in rows or other arrangements on your desk or floor. For example, you might group together related vocabulary items (i.e., family members, hobbies, foods) or parts of speech that follow particular grammatical rules (i.e., strong verbs, weak verbs).

   - Remember that it is rare for there to be a perfect one-to-one correspondence between words in English and German. Make a note of important differences in meaning or usage on the cards.

4. **Examples**—Once you have mastered a new grammatical concept, make up simple statements. Begin by modeling your sentences after the examples in your textbook. Later you will be able to express your own ideas.

5. **Class and videos**—Take notes while you are in class. When your teacher gives you a new example, or if you hear a new phrase while watching a video program, write it down so that you can analyze it at a later time.

6. **Assignment**—Keep up with your assignments. When you are learning a language, you need daily practice and time to absorb new material. Catching up is almost impossible because you can only memorize a certain amount of material at one time.

7. **LANGUAGE LABORATORY**—It is better to listen to tapes for short periods at different times during the week than to try to do everything in one long sitting.

8. **COMPUTER EXERCISES**—These exercises are meant to give you practice and to test your mastery of grammatical rules and concepts. Always review your textbook before beginning computer assignments.

"Viel Glück!"

Cecile Zorach and Charlotte Melin

INTRODUCTION

When you learn a foreign language, in this case German, you need to look at each word in three ways:

1. The **meaning** of the word—You must connect an English word with a German word that has an equivalent meaning.

> *Tree* has basically the same meaning as the German word **Baum**.

Words with equivalent meanings are learned by memorizing vocabulary items. Sometimes two words are the same or very similar in both English and German. These words are called **cognates**. They are especially easy to learn.

German	English
Haus	house
Garten	garden
Student	student
intelligent	intelligent

Sometimes knowing one German word will help you learn another.

> Knowing that **Kellner** is *waiter* should help you learn that **Kellnerin** is *waitress;* or knowing that **wohnen** means *to live* and that **Zimmer** means *room* should help you learn that **Wohnzimmer** means *living room.*

But usually there is little similarity between words, and knowing one German word will not help you learn another. In general, you must learn each vocabulary item separately.

> Knowing that **Mann** means *man* will not help you learn that **Frau** means *woman.*

Even words that have the same basic meaning in English and German only rarely have identical meanings in all situations.

> The German word **Mann** generally has the same meaning as the English word *man,* but it can also mean *husband.* The German word **Frau** usually means *woman*, but it can also mean a married woman, *Mrs.,* or even *Ms.*

In addition, there are times when words in combination take on a special meaning.

> The German word **stehen** means *to stand*; **Schlange** basically means *snake.* But **Schlange stehen** means *to stand in line, to line up.*

An expression whose meaning as a whole (**Schlange stehen**) differs from the meaning of the individual words (**stehen** and **Schlange**) is called an **idiom**. You will need to pay special attention to these idiomatic expressions in order to recognize them and use them correctly.

2. The **classification** of a word—English and German words are classified in categories called **parts of speech**. We will consider the eight different parts of speech used in German:

noun	article
pronoun	adverb
verb	preposition
adjective	conjunction

Each part of speech has its own rules for spelling and use. You must learn to identify the part of speech of each word so that you can choose the correct German equivalent and know what rules to apply.

Look at the word *that* in the following sentences:

    a. Have you read *that* newspaper?
    b. She said *that* she was busy.
    c. Here is the record *that* he bought.[1]

The English word is the same in all three sentences, but in German three different words would be used and three different sets of rules would apply because each *that* is a different part of speech.

3. The **use** of the word—A word must also be identified according to the role it plays in the sentence. Each word, whether English or German, has a specific role or function in the sentence. Determining the word's function will help you choose the correct German equivalent and know what rules apply.

Look at the word *her* in the following sentences:

    a. I don't know *her.*
    b. Have you told *her* your story?
    c. We know *her* father.[2]

The English word is the same in all three sentences, but in German three different words would be used because each *her* has a different function.

[1] a. Adjective-see p. 123; b. Subordinating conjunction-see p. 156; c. Relative pronoun-see p. 114.
[2] a. Direct object-see p. 26; b. Indirect object-see p. 28; c. Possessive adjective-see p. 133.

Careful

As a student of German you must learn to recognize both the part of speech and the function of each word in a given sentence. This is essential because words in a German sentence have a great deal of influence on each other. Compare the following sentence in English and in German.

> *The small blue **book** is on the big old table.*

> Das kleine blaue **Buch** ist auf dem großen alten Tisch.

IN ENGLISH
In English, the only word that affects the form of another word in the sentence is *book*, which causes us to say *is*. If the word were *books*, we would have to say *are*.

IN GERMAN
In German, the word for *book* (**Buch**) not only affects the word for *is* (**ist**), but also the spelling and pronunciation of the German words for *the* (**das**), *small* (**klein**), and *blue* (**blau**). The words for *is on* (**ist auf**) and *table* (**Tisch**) affect the spelling and pronunciation of the equivalent words for *the* (**dem**), *big* (**groß**), and *old* (**alt**). The only word not affected by the words surrounding it is the word for *on* (**auf**).

Since parts of speech and function are usually determined in the same way in English and German, this handbook will show you how to identify them in English. You will then learn to compare English and German constructions. This will give you a better understanding of the explanations in your German textbook.

1. WHAT IS A NOUN?

A **noun** is a word that names something.

IN ENGLISH

Let us look at some different types of words that are nouns:

- a person   friend, sister, brother, John, Mary, Professor Jones
- a place   city, state, country, Austria, New York
- a thing   desk, house, border, water, hand, Monday
- an animal   dog, bird, fish, Spot, Fluff
- an event   vacation, birth, death, jogging, growth
  or activity
- an idea   truth, poverty, inertia, peace, fear, beauty
  or concept

As you can see, a noun can name something tangible, i.e., that you can touch *(door, restaurant, cat)*, or it can refer to something abstract, i.e., something you understand with your mind *(honor, love, justice, humor)*.

A noun that does not state the name of a specific person, place, thing, etc., is called a **common noun**. A common noun begins with a small letter, unless it is the first word of a sentence. All the words above that are not capitalized are common nouns.

A noun that is the name of a specific person, place, thing, etc. is called a **proper noun**. A proper noun always begins with a capital letter. All the words above that are capitalized are proper nouns.

> Her name is Mary.
> | |
> common   proper
>   noun   noun

A noun that is made up of two words is called a **compound noun**. A compound noun can be a common noun, such as *video game* and *ice cream*, or a proper noun, such as *Western Europe* and *North America*.

To help you learn to recognize nouns, here is a paragraph where the nouns are in *italics*.

> The *United States* imports many *items* from German speaking *countries*. German *automobiles*, ranging from moderately priced *models* to elegant *cars*, have earned a *reputation* here for their excellent *performance*. *Germany* also supplies us with fine *tools*,

cameras, and *electronics*. Many *Americans* value imported Swiss *watches*. Nearly everyone in our *country* appreciates the *taste* of Swiss *chocolate*. And some *people* here would feel lost in the *winter* without their *pair* of Austrian *skis*.

IN GERMAN

It is very easy to recognize nouns. German capitalizes all nouns, making no distinction between proper nouns and common nouns.

Terms Used to Talk About Nouns

GENDER—A noun has gender; that is, it can be classified according to whether it is masculine, feminine, or neuter (see **What is Meant by Gender?**, p. 6).

NUMBER—A noun has a number; that is, it can be described as being either singular or plural (see **What is Meant by Number?**, p. 9).

FUNCTION—A noun can have a variety of functions in a sentence; that is, it can be the subject of the sentence (see **What is a Subject?**, p. 24), a predicate noun (see **What is a Predicate Noun?**, p. 32), or an object (see **What are Objects?**, p. 26).

▼▼▼▼▼▼▼▼▼▼▼▼▼▼▼▼▼REVIEW▼▼▼▼▼▼▼▼▼▼▼▼▼▼▼▼▼

Circle the nouns in the following sentences.

1. The student asked the teacher a question.

2. Our textbook has a picture on the cover.

3. Eric wants a new tape deck for his birthday.

4. The cows stood in the middle of a grassy field.

5. Actions speak louder than words.

6. The audience enjoyed her wit and candor.

2. WHAT IS MEANT BY GENDER?

Gender in the grammatical sense means the classification of a word as **masculine, feminine,** or **neuter.**

Gender plays only a small role in English; however, since it is at the very heart of the German language, let us see which parts of speech indicate gender in English and in German.

English	German
pronouns	nouns
possessive adjectives	pronouns
	adjectives
	articles

Since each part of speech follows its own rules to indicate gender, you will find gender discussed in the sections dealing with articles and with the various types of pronouns and adjectives. In this section we shall look at the gender of nouns only.

IN ENGLISH

Nouns themselves do not have gender, but sometimes when they stand for a person or animal, we treat them as if they had grammatical gender, based on their biological sex. If we replace a noun with *he* or *she,* we automatically use *he* for males and *she* for females. Nouns which name things that do not have a sex are replaced by *it.*

Nouns referring to males indicate the masculine gender.

> The *boy* waved; *he* was tired, and I was glad to see *him.*
>   noun   masculine   masculine
>   male

Nouns referring to females indicate the feminine gender.

> My *aunt* came for a visit; *she* is nice and I like *her.*
>   noun   feminine   feminine
>   female

All other nouns do not indicate a gender; they are considered neuter.

> There is a *tree* in front of the house. *It* is a maple.[1]
>   noun   neuter
>   thing

---

[1] There are a few well-known exceptions, such as *ship*, which is referred to as *she*. It is custom, not logic, which decides. "The S/S United States sailed for Europe. *She* is a good ship."

IN GERMAN

All nouns are either masculine, feminine, or neuter. This means that all objects, animals, events, and abstract ideas have a grammatical gender, as do the names of countries.

The gender of most German nouns cannot be explained or figured out. These nouns have a grammatical gender that is unrelated to biological sex. Here are some examples of English nouns classified under the gender of their German equivalents.

Masculine	Feminine	Neuter
table	lamp	window
heaven	hope	girl
tree	plant	bread
month	season	year
state	Switzerland	Germany
beginning	reality	topic

You will have to memorize the grammatical gender of every German noun you learn. This gender is important not only for the noun itself, but also for the spelling and pronunciation of the words it influences.

Gender can sometimes be determined by looking at the ending of a German noun. The list on p. 167 shows you noun endings which signal masculine, feminine, and neuter nouns. You will find it helpful to familiarize yourself with these endings as you learn individual nouns.

Careful

It is easy to determine the grammatical gender of a German noun whose meaning is linked to biological sex (males usually have masculine gender → *Peter, man, brother*; females usually have feminine gender → *Sarah, woman, sister*). A number of nouns, however, have a grammatical gender different from the biological sex of the persons or animals they name. The words for *baby, child*, and *girl* are all neuter because they refer to young or small beings. Often, too, a German noun will have different forms when it refers to the different sexes. For example, the noun "student" has two equivalents, **Studentin** for females and **Student** for males (see Appendix, p. 167). You will want to pay extra attention to such words because it is easy to forget that they have a special grammatical gender in German.

▼▼▼▼▼▼▼▼▼▼▼▼▼▼▼▼▼▼▼REVIEW▼▼▼▼▼▼▼▼▼▼▼▼▼▼▼▼▼▼▼

I. Circle M (masculine), F (feminine), or N (neuter) next to the nouns whose gender you can identify, and (?) next to the nouns whose gender you would have to look up in the dictionary.

1. clock	M	F	N	?
2. mother	M	F	N	?
3. son	M	F	N	?
4. pear	M	F	N	?
5. radio	M	F	N	?

II. By consulting the list on p. 167, determine the gender of the following German words.

1. Lehrer	M	F	N
2. Brötchen	M	F	N
3. Freundin	M	F	N
4. Sonntag	M	F	N
5. Buchhandlung	M	F	N

3. WHAT IS MEANT BY NUMBER?

Number in the grammatical sense means that a word is singular or plural. When a word refers to one person or thing, it is said to be **singular**; when it refers to more than one, it is **plural**.

In German, more parts of speech indicate number than in English, and there are more spelling and pronunciation changes that show number as well. Let us see which parts of speech indicate number in English and German.

English	German
nouns	nouns
verbs	verbs
pronouns	pronouns
only demonstrative adjectives	adjectives
	articles

Since each part of speech follows its own rules to indicate number, you will find number discussed in the sections dealing with articles, the various types of adjectives and pronouns, as well as in all sections on verbs and their tenses. In this section we will look at number in nouns only.

IN ENGLISH

We form the plural of nouns in one of two ways:

1. a singular noun can add an *-s* or *-es*

book	book*s*
kiss	kiss*es*

2. a singular noun can change its spelling

man	m*en*
leaf	lea*ves*
child	child*ren*

A plural noun is usually spelled and pronounced differently from the singular.[1]

Some nouns, called **collective nouns**, refer to a group of persons or things, but the noun itself is considered singular.

A soccer *team* has eleven players.
The *family* is well.
The *crowd* was under control.

---

[1] A few nouns have only one form for both the singular and the plural, i.e., *sheep* → *sheep*.

IN GERMAN

There are several ways of making a singular noun plural. German plurals are less predictable than English ones; they are more like the *man* → *men* or *child* → *children* nouns in English.

Singular	Plural		
Buch	Bücher	*book*	*books*
Wagen	Wagen	*car*	*cars*
Vater	Väter	*father*	*fathers*
Gast	Gäste	*guest*	*guests*
Frau	Frauen	*woman*	*women*

Notice that German can use an **umlaut** (¨) to form plural nouns. This changes both the spelling of the word and its pronunciation. As you learn new nouns in German, you should memorize each noun's gender and its singular and plural forms. Consult the list on p. 167 for some hints about how different genders form their plural.

Note that nouns do not change gender when they become plural.

▼▼▼▼▼▼▼▼▼▼▼▼▼▼▼▼▼REVIEW▼▼▼▼▼▼▼▼▼▼▼▼▼▼▼▼▼

I. Circle the English words that are in the plural.

1. pencils
2. suitcase
3. business
4. feet
5. group

II. Under the "Plural" column, circle the parts of the German word that indicate the plural form.

Singular	Plural
1. Wort	Wörter
2. Stuhl	Stühle
3. Kind	Kinder
4. Student	Studenten
5. Auto	Autos

4. WHAT ARE ARTICLES?

An **article** is a word placed before a noun to show whether the noun refers to a particular person, animal, place, thing, event, or idea, or whether the noun refers to an unspecified person, thing, or idea.

Definite Articles

IN ENGLISH

A **definite article** is used before a noun when we are speaking about a particular person, place, animal, thing, or idea. There is one definite article, *the*.

> I read *the* book you recommended.
> a particular book

> I ate *the* apple you gave me.
> a particular apple

The definite article remains *the* when the noun it precedes becomes plural.

> I read *the books* you recommended.
> I ate *the apples* you gave me.

IN GERMAN

As in English, a definite article is used before a noun when we refer to a particular person, place, animal, thing, or idea. You will have to pay much more attention to German articles than to their English counterparts, however, because they must match the noun to which they belong. This "matching" is called **agreement** (we say that "the article *agrees* with the noun"). To choose the correct form of the article, you must know the following information about the noun to which it belongs: gender, number, and case.

To introduce you to articles, we will give you only the basic form of the article as you will find it in your textbook vocabulary list or in the dictionary. In the chapter **What is Meant by Case?**, p. 15, you will see how these forms change according to the article's function in a sentence. There are four forms of the definite article: three singular forms and one plural.

Der indicates that the noun is masculine singular.

> **der** Baum   *the tree*

Die indicates that the noun is feminine singular.

> **die** Tür   *the door*

Das indicates that the noun is neuter singular.

> **das** Haus   *the house*

Die is also the plural definite article. In the plural, the gender of the noun is not important because the article **die** is used with masculine, feminine, and neuter plural nouns.

> **die** Türen   *the doors*

Since the same definite article **die** is used for plural nouns and for feminine singular nouns, you will have to rely on other indicators to determine the number of the noun. The most common indicator is the form of the noun itself: is it the singular form or the plural form?

> **die** Tür   *the door*
> |
> singular
> **die** → feminine singular

> **die** Türen   *the doors*
> |
> plural
> **die** → plural

You will discover other indicators of number as you learn more German (see **What is Meant by Case?**, p. 15, and **What is a Verb Conjugation?**, p. 57).

Indefinite Articles

IN ENGLISH
An **indefinite article** is used before a noun when we are speaking about an unspecified person, animal, place, thing, event, or idea. There are two indefinite articles, *a* and *an*.

A is used before a word beginning with a consonant.

> I saw *a* boy in the street.
> |
> not a particular boy

An is used before a word beginning with a vowel.

I ate *an* apple.
not a particular apple

The indefinite article is used only with a singular noun. When the noun becomes plural, we omit it or replace it with the word *some*.

I saw boys in the street.
I saw *some* boys in the street.

I ate apples.
I ate *some* apples.

IN GERMAN

An indefinite article is used in German before a noun that refers to an unspecified person, animal, place, thing, event, or idea. Indefinite articles, like definite articles, must agree with the noun in gender, number, and case. As in English, the indefinite article is used only with a singular noun. There are two forms of the indefinite article.

Ein indicates that the noun is masculine or neuter.

ein Baum   *a tree*
    masculine

ein Haus   *a house*
    neuter

Eine indicates that the noun is feminine.

eine Tür   *a door*
    feminine

Your German textbook will discuss the different forms of the definite and indefinite articles in greater detail.

▼▼▼▼▼▼▼▼▼▼▼▼▼▼▼▼▼▼REVIEW▼▼▼▼▼▼▼▼▼▼▼▼▼▼▼▼▼▼

I. Here is a list of German nouns as they appear in a dictionary. The dictionary entry indicates whether the noun is masculine *(m.)*, feminine *(f.)*, or neuter *(n.)*. Write the German definite article for each noun in the space provided.

Article	**Dictionary entry**
1. _____	Bett, *n.*
2. _____	Woche, *f.*
3. _____	Kugelschreiber, *m.*
4. _____	Uhr, *f.*
5. _____	Heft, *n.*

II. The following is a list of German nouns preceded by definite and indefinite articles, together with their English equivalents. Write the appropriate English article in the space provided.

1. die Straße   _____ street

2. ein Bleistift   _____ pencil

3. der Zug   _____ train

4. ein Zimmer   _____ room

5. das Wetter   _____ weather

5. WHAT IS MEANT BY CASE?

Case indicates how certain words function within a sentence. The case of a word is shown by the particular form of the word itself or by the form of the words that accompany it.

Case is very important in German because it affects the form of several parts of speech. Let us look at how case is indicated in English and German.

English
form of pronouns

German
form of nouns
form of pronouns
form of adjectives
form of articles

IN ENGLISH

The function of nouns in a sentence, and therefore the meaning of the sentence, is indicated by the order of the words in the sentence. We easily recognize the difference in meaning between the following two sentences purely on the basis of word order. The nouns themselves remain the same even though they serve different functions in the two sentences:

> The girl gives the teacher the apple.
>
>> Here the girl is giving
>> and the teacher is receiving.
>
> The teacher gives the girl the apple.
>
>> Here the teacher is giving
>> and the girl is receiving.

If we begin moving the words around, we can make up nonsense sentences:

> The apple is giving the teacher the girl.
> The girl is giving the apple the teacher.

These sentences show how we can completely change the meaning of an English sentence by changing the position, and therefore the function, of the nouns.

Case of English Pronouns

The function of pronouns in English is indicated not only by word order but also by case (see **What is a Personal Pronoun?**, p. 40). In the two examples below, it is not only word order but also the form, i.e., the case, of the pronoun that affects the sentence's meaning:

>*I* know *them.*
>*They* know *me.*

We cannot say, "I know *they*" or "They know *I*" because the forms "they" and "I" cannot be used as objects of a verb (see **What are Objects?**, p. 26). If you learn to recognize the different cases of pronouns in English you will find it easier to understand the German case system.

English pronouns have three cases:

1. The **nominative case** is used when a pronoun is a subject or a predicate nominative. Predicate nominatives are discussed in a separate section on predicate nouns. (See **What is a Subject?**, p. 24 and **What is a Predicate Noun?**, p. 32.)

   > *She* and *I* went to the movies.
   >
   > subjects →
   > nominative

   > *We* enjoyed the film.
   >
   > subject →
   > nominative

   > It was *he* who did the deed.
   >
   > predicate →
   > nominative

2. The **objective case** is used when a pronoun is a direct object, an indirect object, or an object of a preposition (see **What are Objects?**, p. 26).

   > *They* invited both *him* and *me.*
   >
   > subject →   direct objects →
   > nominative   objective

   > *They* sent *us* a note.
   >
   > subject →   indirect object →
   > nominative   objective

   > *We* asked about *them.*
   >
   > subject →   object of preposition →
   > nominative   objective

In these examples, the form of the pronoun changes because the pronoun has different functions in the sentences. *We* and *us* refer to the same people, but *we* can only function as the subject of a sentence. (You can't say "*Us* went to the movies.") *They* and *them* refer to the same people, but *they* can only function as the subject of a sentence. (You can't say "*Them* asked about me.") *They* and *them* are different cases of the same pronoun, as are *we* and *us*, *she* and *her*, *he* and *him*, and *I* and *me*.

3. The **possessive case** is used when a pronoun shows ownership. The possessive pronoun can function as subject, predicate noun, direct object, indirect object, or object of a preposition.

> Is this book *yours*?
> |
>   possessive →
>   predicate noun

> Kit called her parents, but I wrote *mine* a letter.
> |
>   possessive →
>   indirect object

> Mary has finished her test, but John is still working on *his*.
> |
>   possessive →
>   object of preposition

The possessive case is discussed in a separate section (see **What is a Possessive Pronoun?**, p. 100).

IN GERMAN

Word order does not indicate the function of nouns within a sentence. Instead, the function of a noun is indicated by either the form of the noun itself or the form of its definite or indefinite article. These different forms indicate case. As long as the nouns are put in their proper cases, the words in the sentence can be moved around without changing the essential meaning of the sentence. Look at the many ways a sentence can be expressed in German.

> *The girl gives the teacher the apple.*
>
> **Das** Mädchen gibt **dem** Lehrer **den** Apfel.
> *the girl   gives to the teacher the apple*
>
> **Dem** Lehrer gibt **das** Mädchen **den** Apfel.
> *to the teacher gives the girl   the apple*
>
> **Den** Apfel gibt **das** Mädchen **dem** Lehrer.
> *the apple   gives the girl   to the teacher*

The different case endings on the articles **das, dem** and **den** *(the)* show the function of the words in the sentence: **das Mädchen** *(the girl)* must be the subject of the sentence and, therefore, the girl is doing the giving; **den Apfel** *(the apple)* is the direct object and, therefore, the apple is the object given; **dem Lehrer** *(the teacher)* is the indirect object and, therefore, the teacher is the person to whom the apple is given. The different word order in all three sentences simply shows what part of the sentence the speaker wants to emphasize.

Case of German Nouns

German has four different cases for nouns, each reflecting a different function of the word in the sentence.

1. the nominative
2. the accusative
3. the dative
4. the genitive

Each case has a singular and plural form (see **What is Meant by Number?**, p. 9). The complete set of case forms for any noun (indicated primarily by the endings given to the accompanying article) is called the noun's **declension**. When you have memorized these forms, you are able to "decline" that noun. Let us look at a set of noun declensions in German.

	Masculine	**SINGULAR** **Feminine**	**Neuter**	**PLURAL**
nominative	**der** Apfel	**die** Tür	**das** Kind	**die** Bücher
accusative	**den** Apfel	**die** Tür	**das** Kind	**die** Bücher
dative	**dem** Apfel	**der** Tür	**dem** Kind	**den** Büchern
genitive	**des** Apfels	**der** Tür	**des** Kindes	**der** Bücher

As you can see, case affects the form of the noun itself only in the masculine and neuter genitive singular and in the plural dative.[1] The definite article that accompanies the noun also reflects the case of the noun and changes its form according to how the noun functions in a sentence.

When you memorize a declension, you will learn the following cases:

---

[1]A small group of nouns, called **weak nouns**, have different forms to indicate case. Your textbook will explain their declension together with other exceptions.

1. The **nominative case** is used for the subject of a sentence and for predicate nouns. (See **What is a Subject?**, p. 24 and **What is a Predicate Noun?**, p. 32.) This is the form of nouns listed in a vocabulary list or a dictionary.

2. The **accusative case** is used for most direct objects. (See **What are Objects?**, p. 26.)

3. The **dative case** is used for indirect objects and for the object of a few verbs that you will have to memorize.

4. The **genitive case** is used to show possession or close relation. (See **What is the Possessive?**, p. 34.)

The accusative, dative, and occasionally the genitive case are used as the objects of prepositions. (See **What is a Preposition?**, p. 141.)

To show you how a change in case leads to a change in meaning, let us take the sentence used above, "The girl gives the teacher the apple," and change it to mean "The teacher gives the girl the apple." We can do this by simply changing the case of the nouns in German. Once again the definite articles indicate the different functions of the nouns.

The girl gives the teacher the apple.
Das Mädchen gibt dem Lehrer den Apfel.

    nominative   dative   accusative

the girl   gives to the teacher   the apple

The teacher gives the girl the apple.
Der Lehrer gibt dem Mädchen den Apfel.

nominative   dative   accusative

the teacher   gives to the girl   the apple

To choose the appropriate case for each noun in the second German sentence, you need to go through a series of steps:

The teacher gives the girl the apple.

1. Identify the gender and number of each noun.

       teacher → **der Lehrer** → masculine singular
       girl → **das Mädchen** → neuter singular
       apple → **der Apfel** → masculine singular

2. Determine how each noun functions in the sentence.

> teacher → subject
> girl → indirect object
> apple → direct object

3. Determine what case in German corresponds to the function you have identified in step 2.

> teacher → subject → nominative case
> girl → indirect object → dative case
> apple → direct object → accusative case

4. Choose the proper form from the declension you have memorized.

> Der Lehrer gibt dem Mädchen den Apfel.

masculine	neuter	masculine
singular	singular	singular
nominative	dative	accusative

Your textbook will show you the different case forms for the definite and indefinite articles and explain how to use them. As you learn more German, you will discover other ways in which case affects the form of nouns, pronouns, and adjectives (see **What is a Personal Pronoun?**, p. 40, and **What is an Adjective?**, p. 123).

▼▼▼▼▼▼▼▼▼▼▼▼▼▼▼▼REVIEW▼▼▼▼▼▼▼▼▼▼▼▼▼▼▼▼

In the following English sentences, circle the words that will be affected by case in a German sentence.

1. The children ran after the ball.

2. When the cat is away, the mice will play.

3. A car pulled out of the drive.

4. An insider leaked the story to the press.

5. The end of the movie was a surprise.

6. WHAT IS A VERB?

A **verb** is a word that expresses "the action" of the sentence. Here the word "action" is used in its broadest sense and is not necessarily limited to physical action.

IN ENGLISH

Verbs can express many different types of action:

- a physical activity   to run, to walk, to hit, to sit
- a mental activity   to dream, to think, to believe, to hope
- a condition   to be, to become, to seem

Many verbs, however, do not fall neatly into one of these categories. They are still verbs because they represent "the action" of the sentence.

> The book *costs* $5.00.
> |
>   to cost

> I *have* a cold.
> |
>   to have

To help you learn to recognize verbs, here is a paragraph where the verbs are in *italics*.

> The three students *entered* the restaurant, *selected* a table, *hung* up their coats and *sat* down. They *looked* at the menu and *asked* the waitress what she *recommended*. She *suggested* the daily special, roast chicken. It *was* not expensive. They *chose* a bottle of white wine and *ordered* a salad. The service *was* slow, but the food *tasted* excellent. Good cooking, they *decided, takes* time. They *ate* strudel for dessert and *finished* the meal with coffee.

The verb is one of the most important words of a sentence; you cannot write a **complete sentence**, i.e., express a complete thought without a verb. It is important for you to learn to identify verbs because the function of many words in a sentence depends on their relationship to the verb. For example, the subject of a sentence performs the action of the verb and the object receives the action of the verb (see **What is a Subject?**, p. 24 and **What are Objects?**, p. 26).

IN GERMAN
Verbs are identified the same way as they are in English.

Transitive and Intransitive Verbs

There are two types of verbs in both English and German: transitive and intransitive.

A **transitive verb** is a verb that takes a direct object. It is indicated by the abbreviation *v.t.* (verb transitive) in dictionaries.

> The boy *threw* the ball.
> | |
> transitive direct object

> She *lost* her job.
> | |
> transitive direct object

An **intransitive verb** is a verb that cannot take a direct object. It is indicated by the abbreviation *v.i.* (verb intransitive) in dictionaries.

> Laura *arrives* today.
> | |
> intransitive adverb

> Brian *is sleeping*.
> |_____|
>   intransitive

Many verbs can be used both transitively and intransitively, but in every case the above distinction remains true: transitive usage permits a direct object, and intransitive usage does not.

> The students *speak* German.
> | |
>   transitive direct object

> Actions *speak* louder than words.
> | |_____|
>   intransitive adverbial phrase

Some verbs that are transitive in English are intransitive in German, while other verbs that are intransitive in English are transitive in German. You will find several examples of how verbs function differently in German and in English in the sections **What are Objects?**, p. 26 and **What is a Reflexive Verb?**, p. 106.

Terms Used to Talk About Verbs

INFINITIVE—The verb form which is the name of the verb is called an infinitive: *to eat, to sleep, to drink* (see **What is an Infinitive?**, p. 55).

CONJUGATION—A verb is conjugated or changes in form to agree with its subject: *I do, she does* (see **What is a Verb Conjugation?**, p. 57).

TENSE—A verb indicates tense, that is, the time (present, past, or future) of the action: *I am, I was, I will be* (see **What is Meant by Tense?**, p. 62).

VOICE—A verb shows voice, that is, the relation between the subject and the action of the verb (see **What is Meant by Active and Passive Voice?**, p. 150).

MOOD—A verb shows moods, that is, the speaker's attitude toward what he or she is saying (see **What is Meant by Mood?**, p. 86).

PARTICIPLE—A verb may also be used to form a participle (see **What is a Participle?**, p. 71).

▼▼▼▼▼▼▼▼▼▼▼▼▼▼▼▼REVIEW▼▼▼▼▼▼▼▼▼▼▼▼▼▼▼▼

Circle the verbs in the following sentences.

1. The students eat their lunch at school.

2. Robin and Jeff met at the library.

3. We stayed home because we expected a phone call.

4. Rachel took a bath, finished her novel, and went to bed.

5. Sam felt better after he talked to his friends.

7. WHAT IS A SUBJECT?

The **subject** of a sentence is the person or thing that performs the action of the verb.[1]

IN ENGLISH

To find the subject of a sentence, look for the verb first (see **What is a Verb?**, p. 21); then ask, *who?* or *what?* before the verb. The answer will be the subject.

> Peter studies German.
>> Who studies German? Peter.
>> *Peter* is the subject.
>> (Note that the subject is singular. It refers to one person.)

> Did the packages come yesterday?
>> What came yesterday? The packages.
>> *The packages* is the subject.
>> (Note that the subject is plural. It refers to more than one thing.)

Train yourself to ask this question to find the subject. Never assume a word is the subject because it comes first in the sentence. Subjects can be located in several different places, as you can see in the following examples (the **subject** is in boldface and the *verb* italicized):

> After running 26 miles, **Ann** *was* very tired.
> Standing at the top of the stairs *was* a tall **man**.

Some sentences have more than one main verb; you must find the subject of each verb.

> The **boys** *were doing* the cooking while **Mary** *was setting* the table.
>> **Boys** is the plural subject of *were doing*.
>> **Mary** is the singular subject of *was setting*.

IN GERMAN

It is particularly important that you recognize the subject of a sentence so that you put it in the proper case (see **What is meant by Case?**, p. 15). The subject of a German sentence is in the nominative case.

---

[1]The subject performs the action in an active sentence, but is acted upon in a passive sentence (see **What is Meant by Active and Passive Voice?**, p. 150).

Das Kind spielt allein.
nominative
3rd person singular neuter
The child is playing alone.

Wir kommen spät.
nominative
1st person plural
We are coming late.

Petra und **Franz** arbeiten heute.
nominative
3rd person plural
Petra and Franz are working today.

In English and in German it is very important to find the subject of each verb so that you can choose the form of the verb that goes with the subject (see **What is a Verb Conjugation?**, p. 57).

▼▼▼▼▼▼▼▼▼▼▼▼▼▼▼▼▼REVIEW▼▼▼▼▼▼▼▼▼▼▼▼▼▼▼▼▼

Find the subjects in the following English sentences.
■ Next to Q write the question you need to ask to find the subject.
■ Next to A write the answer to the question you asked.

1. The bus leaves in fifteen minutes.

Q: _____

A: _____

2. When the game was over, everyone went home.

Q: _____

A: _____

Q:_____

A: _____

3. My friends and I took a boat ride down the Rhine.

Q: _____

A: _____

8. WHAT ARE OBJECTS?

Every sentence consists, at the very least, of a subject and a verb.

> Children play.
> Work stopped.

The subject of the sentence is usually a noun (see **What is a Noun?**, p. 4) or a pronoun (see **What is a Personal Pronoun?**, p. 40). Many sentences contain other nouns or pronouns that are related to the action of the verb or to a preposition. We call these nouns or pronouns **objects**.

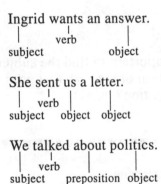

We will study three types of objects: the direct object, indirect object, and object of a preposition.

Direct Object

IN ENGLISH

A **direct object** is a noun or pronoun that receives the action of the verb or shows the result of that action directly, without a preposition.[1] It answers the question *what?* or *whom?* asked after the verb.

> Paula reads *the book.*
>> Paula reads what? The book.
>> *The book* is the direct object.

> They are inviting *Paula* and *her sister.*
>> They are inviting whom? Paula and her sister.
>> *Paula* and *her sister* are the two direct objects.

---

[1]In this section, we will consider only active sentences (see **What is Meant by Active and Passive Voice?**, p. 150).

Never assume that a word that comes right after a verb is the direct object. It must answer the question *what?* or *whom?*

John writes well.

> John writes *what*? No answer.
> John writes *whom*? No answer.

There is no direct object in this sentence. *Well* is an adverb; it answers the question "John write *how?*" (See **What is an Adverb?**, p. 139).

IN GERMAN

Objects are divided into categories depending on their case, mainly accusative and dative (see **What is Meant by Case?**, p. 15). An object will never be in the nominative, and you will rarely encounter an object in the genitive. Most English direct objects are expressed by the accusative case in German.

> *Paula reads **the book**.*
> Paula reads what? The book.
> *The book* is the direct object.

Paula liest **das Buch**.
subject   neuter singular
              direct object → accusative

> *They are inviting **Paula** and **her sister**.*
> They are inviting whom? Paula and her sister.
> *Paula* and *her sister* are the direct objects.

Sie laden **Paula** und **ihre Schwester** ein.
subject   direct objects → accusative

A few common German verbs require a dative object even though their English equivalents have direct objects. Your German textbook will tell you about these verbs, and you will need to memorize them. Here are two examples:

> *They thank **the policeman**.*
> They thank whom? The policeman.
> *The policeman* is the direct object.

Sie danken **dem Polizisten**.
subject   dative object
> The verb **danken** *(to thank)* requires a dative object.

We are helping you.
> We are helping whom? You.
> *You* is the direct object.

Wir helfen **dir**.
| |
subject   dative object

> The verb **helfen** *(to help)* requires a dative object.

Indirect Object

IN ENGLISH

An **indirect object** is a noun or pronoun that receives the action of the verb or shows the result of that action indirectly. It explains "to whom," "to what," "for whom," or "for what" the action of the verb is done. It answers the question *to whom, for whom?* or *to what, for what?* asked after the verb.

John writes *his brother.*

> John writes to whom? To his brother.
> *His brother* is the indirect object.

Susan did *me* a favor.

> Susan did a favor for whom? For me.
> *Me* is the indirect object.

IN GERMAN

Most English indirect objects are expressed by the dative case in German.

*John writes **his brother**.*
> John writes to whom? His brother.
> *His brother* is the indirect object.

John schreibt **seinem Bruder**.
| |
subject   dative object

*Susan did **me** a favor.*
> Susan did a favor for whom? Me.
> *Me* is the indirect object.

Susan tat **mir** einen Gefallen.
| | |
subject   dative   accusative
          object   object

Sentences with a Direct and an Indirect Object

Many verbs in English and in German have both direct and indirect objects. Let us look at an example to see how to recognize the two types of objects:

We *gave* **the postman the letter**.
subject verb   indirect   direct
            object   object

We gave what? The letter.
The letter is the direct object.

We gave the letter to whom? To the postman.
The postman is the indirect object.

Wir gaben **dem Briefträger den Brief**.
subject   verb   dative   accusative
            indirect   direct
            object   object

Often the indirect object in an English sentence is expressed using the preposition *to* or *for*. We could say, for example, "We gave the letter to the postman." Notice that *the postman* is still the indirect object.

Object of a Preposition

IN ENGLISH

The noun or pronoun which follows a preposition is called the **object of the preposition**. It answers the question *what?* or *whom?* asked after the preposition (see **What is a Preposition?**, p. 141).

The book is in *the desk*.

The book is in what? In the desk.
The desk is the object of the preposition *in*.

John is working for *Gretchen*.

John is working for whom? For Gretchen.
Gretchen is the object of the preposition *for*.

IN GERMAN

Objects of a preposition are as easy to identify as they are in English. German prepositions, however, have objects in particular cases, usually accusative or dative, and sometimes genitive. As you memorize prepositions, you will need to learn which case each preposition takes. For example, here are three different prepositions, each requiring a different case.

um diese Stadt
accusative with **um**
around this city

von solchen Büchern
dative with **von**
about such books

wegen des Sturmes
genitive with **wegen**
on account of the storm

Careful

As a student of German you must watch out for the following pitfalls:

An English verb that requires a preposition before its object may have a German equivalent that simply requires an accusative.

> *She is looking for her coat.*
>> She is looking for what? Her coat.
>> *Her coat* is the object of the preposition *for*.
>
> Sie sucht **ihren Mantel**.
>> accusative object
>> The verb **suchen** is the equivalent of *to look for* and takes an accusative object.

The preposition that follows a German verb may be different from the preposition that follows an English verb.

> *He is waiting for his friend.*
> Er wartet **auf** seinen Freund.
>> literally, *on*

> *I am asking you for advice.*
> Ich bitte dich **um** Rat.
>> literally, *about*

Your German textbook will introduce phrases like **warten auf** +
accusative object *(to wait for)* and **bitten um** + accusative object *(to
ask for)*. Make sure you learn the verb together with the preposition
and its case so that you can use the entire pattern correctly. Remember
that German is a separate language with structures different from English and avoid the error of translating word-for-word from English
into German.

▼▼▼▼▼▼▼▼▼▼▼▼▼▼▼▼▼REVIEW▼▼▼▼▼▼▼▼▼▼▼▼▼▼▼▼▼

The following sentences contain different types of objects.
- Next to Q write the question you need to ask to find the object.
- Next to A write the answer to the question you just asked.
- In the column to the right, identify the kind of object you found by circling
  the appropriate letters: direct object (DO), indirect object (IO), or object of
  a preposition (OP).

1. The computer lost my homework.

Q: _____   DO   IO   OP

A: _____

2. She sent her friend a postcard.

Q: _____   DO   IO   OP

A: _____

Q: _____   DO   IO   OP

A: _____

3. My parents paid for the books with a credit card.

Q: _____   DO   IO   OP

A: _____

Q: _____   DO   IO   OP

A: _____

9. WHAT IS A PREDICATE NOUN?

A **predicate noun** is a noun in a sentence that refers to the same thing as the subject of the sentence.

```
        same person
     ┌─────────┴─────────┐
    Mary is a girl.
     │          │
   subject   predicate noun
```

A predicate noun is connected to the subject by a **linking verb**, a verb which *links* interchangeable elements, that acts like an equal sign. In the sentence above, the verb *is* links *Mary* to *girl* (Mary = girl).

IN ENGLISH

The most common linking verbs in English are *to be* and *to become*. Although these verbs often have a noun after them in the sentence, this noun does not receive the action of the verb and is not a direct object (see **What are Objects?**, p. 26); instead it is interchangeable with the subject and is called a **predicate noun**.

```
    Mary is a good student.
     │    │            │
     │  linking verb   │
   subject        predicate noun
```

```
    John became a teacher.
     │      │         │
     │  linking verb  │
   subject       predicate noun
```

IN GERMAN

Predicate nouns are in the nominative case because they point to the subject, which is also in the nominative case (see **What is Meant by Case?**, p. 15).

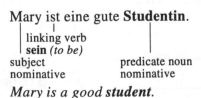

```
    Mary ist eine gute Studentin.
     │    │                  │
     │  linking verb         │
     │  sein (to be)         │
   subject            predicate noun
   nominative         nominative
```
*Mary is a good **student**.*

John wurde **Lehrer**.

```
  |          |
  | linking verb
  | werden (to become)|
subject          predicate noun
nominative       nominative
```

John became a teacher.

You should learn to recognize linking verbs like **sein** *(to be)*, **werden** *(to become)*, and **scheinen** *(to appear)*, which often have a predicate noun following them.

▼▼▼▼▼▼▼▼▼▼▼▼▼▼▼▼▼REVIEW▼▼▼▼▼▼▼▼▼▼▼▼▼▼▼▼▼▼

Circle the predicate noun in the following sentences.
- Draw an arrow from the the subject to the predicate noun to which it refers.

1. The letter was really good news.

2. Carol became a doctor.

3. They are tourists.

4. Dan became an accomplished musician.

5. The swimming pool is our favorite place in the summer.

10. WHAT IS THE POSSESSIVE?

The **possessive** is used to show that one noun *possesses* or owns another noun, or that the two nouns have a similar, close relation to each other.

IN ENGLISH
You can show possession in one of two ways:

1. An apostrophe can be used. In this construction, the noun possessor comes before the noun possessed.

   ▪ a singular common or proper noun adds an apostrophe + "s"

      > Inge*'s* mother
      > the child*'s* ball
      > the professor*'s* book
      > |
      > singular possessor

   ▪ a plural possessor ending with "s" adds an apostrophe

      > the girl*s'* father
      > the boy*s'* school
      > |
      > plural possessor

   ▪ a plural possessor not ending with "s" adds an apostrophe + "s"

      > the children*'s* playground
      > the women*'s* role
      > |
      > plural possessor

2. The word *of* can be used. In this construction, the noun possessed comes before the noun possessor.

   ▪ a proper noun possessor is preceded by *of*

      > the poetry *of* Goethe
      > |
      > proper noun possessor

   ▪ a singular or plural common noun possessor is precede by *of the* or *of a (an)*

      > the branches *of a* tree
      > the book *of the* professor
      > the teacher *of the* students
      > |
      > common noun possessor

IN GERMAN
There are also two ways of showing possession.

1. The genitive case can be used. This case is formed as follows:

PROPER NOUNS
- most proper nouns add "-s"

>   Inges Mutter
>   *Inge's mother*
>   ⌐   ⌐
>   possessor possessed

>   Goethes Dichtung
>   *Goethe's poetry*

- proper nouns ending in "-s" or "-z" add an apostrophe

>   Kiwus' Gedichte
>   *Kiwus's poems*
>   ⌐   ⌐
>   possessor possessed

With proper nouns, the possessor comes before the thing possessed, just as in English.

COMMON NOUNS—The genitive case is indicated differently depending on whether the common noun is masculine, feminine or neuter, singular or plural.

- most masculine and neuter singular nouns of one syllable add "-**es**". The accompanying articles likewise end in "-s".

>   der Ball des Kindes
>   ⌐   ⌐
>   possessed   possessor
>   *ball*   *child*
>   neuter singular
>   one syllable **Kind**
>   genitive
>   definite article
>   *the child's ball*

- most masculine and neuter singular nouns of more than one syllable add "-s". The accompanying articles likewise end in "-s".

>   das Buch des Professors
>   ⌐
>   possessor
>   *professor*
>   masculine singular
>   more than one syllable
>   *the professor's book*

- feminine singular and plural nouns have no special genitive ending. To indicate possession, you add **-er** to the preceding article or adjectives.

der Mantel d**er Frau**
| feminine singular
*the **woman's** coat*

der Vater d**er Mädchen**
| neuter plural
*the **girls'** father*

Kisten alt**er Bücher**
| neuter plural
*boxes of **old books***

With common nouns, the possessor generally follows the thing possessed. The German structure parallels the English structure using *of the* (see p. 34). Your German textbook will explain the genitive in greater detail and will point out a few irregularities that occur.

2. The word **von** + the dative case can be used. This construction occurs with proper and common nouns and corresponds to using *of* to express possession in English.

die Mutter **von** Inge
*the mother **of** Inge*

die Dichtung **von** Goethe
*the poetry **of** Goethe*

der Motor **vom** Auto
| von + dem
*the motor **of the** car*

der Vater **von den** Mädchen
*the father **of the** girls*

In general, **von** + the dative is used to express possession in colloquial German while the genitive case is used in writing and in formal language.

▼▼▼▼▼▼▼▼▼▼▼▼▼▼▼▼REVIEW▼▼▼▼▼▼▼▼▼▼▼▼▼▼▼▼

The following are possessive constructions using the apostrophe.
- Write the alternate English structure using the word *of*.
- Underline the possessor in your new construction.

1. the car's motor

_____

2. a test's results

_____

3. the year's end

_____

4. two cities' tale

_____

5. Bachmann's works

_____

11. WHAT IS A PRONOUN?

A **pronoun** is a word used in place of one or more nouns. It may stand, therefore, for a person, place, thing, or idea (see **What is a Noun?**, p. 4).

For example, rather than repeating the proper noun "Karen" in the following two sentences, it sounds more natural to use a pronoun in the second sentence.

> Karen likes to sing. Karen practices every day.
> Karen likes to sing. *She* practices every day.

Generally a pronoun is used to refer to someone (or something) that has already been mentioned. The word that the pronoun replaces is called the **antecedent** of the pronoun. In the example above, the pronoun *she* refers to the proper noun *Karen*. *Karen* is the antecedent of the pronoun *she*.

IN ENGLISH

There are different types of pronouns, each serving a different function and following different rules. The list below presents the most important types and refers you to the section where they are discussed.

PERSONAL PRONOUNS—These pronouns refer to different persons (i.e., *me, you, her*) and they change their form according to the function they have in a sentence (see p. 40). The personal pronouns include:

SUBJECT PRONOUNS—These pronouns are used as the subject of a verb (see p. 40).

> *I* go.
> *They* read.
> *He* runs.

OBJECT PRONOUNS—These pronouns can be used as:

- a direct object (see p. 43)

> Jane loves *him*.
> Mark saw *them* at the theater.

- an indirect object (see p. 43)

> The boy wrote *me* the letter.
> Petra gave *us* the book.

- an object of a preposition (see p. 48)

> Angela is going to the movies with *us*.
> Don't step on it; walk around *it*.

REFLEXIVE PRONOUNS—These pronouns refer back to the subject of the sentence (see p. 102).

>I cut *myself.*
>She spoke about *herself.*

INTERROGATIVE PRONOUNS—These pronouns are used in questions (see p. 108).

>*Who* is that?
>*What* do you want?

POSSESSIVE PRONOUNS—These pronouns are used to show possession (see p. 100).

>Whose book is that? *Mine.*
>*Yours* is on the table.

RELATIVE PRONOUNS—These pronouns are used to introduce relative subordinate clauses (see p. 114).

>The man *who* came is very nice.
>Meg, *whom* you met, wants to study in Berlin.

IN GERMAN

Pronouns are identified in the same way as in English. The most important difference is that German pronouns use more case forms than English pronouns (see **What is Meant by Case?**, p. 15). German pronouns must also agree in gender and number with the nouns they replace; that is, they must correspond in gender and number to their antecedents (see **What is Meant by Gender?**, p. 6, and **What is Meant by Number?**, p. 9).

▼▼▼▼▼▼▼▼▼▼▼▼▼▼▼▼▼REVIEW▼▼▼▼▼▼▼▼▼▼▼▼▼▼▼▼▼▼

Circle the pronouns in the sentences below.
■ Draw an arrow from the pronoun to its antecedent(s).

1. Did Brooke phone? Yes, she called a few minutes ago.

2. Molly and Stan were out. They had a lot of errands to run.

3. If the paper is not next to the chair, look under it.

4. Jim baked the cake himself.

5. Has Brad met Helga yet? Yes, Brad already knows her.

12. WHAT IS A PERSONAL PRONOUN?

Both in English and in German, we use **personal pronouns** to refer to different persons or things. Here are some examples:

I (me)	used by the person or persons speaking;
we (us)	called **1st person pronouns**
you	used for the person or persons spoken to;
	called **2nd person pronouns**
he (him), she (her)	used for the person or persons,
it, they (them)	or thing or things spoken about;
	called **3rd person pronouns**

These personal pronouns (except *you*) clearly indicate number; that is, they show whether one person or more than one is involved. *I* and *she,* for example, are singular pronouns, *we* and *they* are plural (see **What is Meant by Number?**, p. 9).

In both German and English, a personal pronoun has different forms to show its function in a sentence; these forms are called **case forms** (see **What is Meant by Case?**, p. 15). For example, *we* and *us* are different cases of the 1st person plural pronoun. Personal pronouns can function as subjects, objects, and objects of prepositions. These functions are discussed below.

Personal Pronouns as Subjects

In the following examples a personal pronoun is used as the subject of a verb (see **What is a Subject?**, p. 24).

> *They* ran, but *I* walked.
>
>> Who ran? They.
>> *They* is the subject of the verb *ran*.
>
>> Who walked? I.
>> *I* is the subject of the verb *walked*.

Let us compare the subject pronouns in English and German. In both languages, the form of the pronoun used for the subject is called the **nominative case**. Although the case system is much more developed in German than in English, understanding the cases of pronouns in English can help you understand how cases work in German.

ENGLISH nominative case		GERMAN nominative case	
Singular			
I	1st person *the person speaking*	**ich**	
you	2nd person *the person spoken to*	{ **du** **Sie**	familiar formal
he she it	3rd person *the person or thing spoken about*	{ **er** **sie** **es**	masculine feminine neuter
Plural			
we	1st person *the person speaking + others* Mary and I speak German. we	**wir**	
you	2nd person *the persons spoken to* Mary and you speak German. you plural	{ **ihr** **Sie**	familiar formal
they	3rd person *the persons or things spoken about* Mary and John speak German. they	**sie**	

As you can see from the chart above, two subject pronouns in English have more than one equivalent in German: *you* and *it*. Let us look more closely at these two subject pronouns.

"You"—du, ihr, *or* Sie?

IN ENGLISH

You is always used to address another person or persons. We use the same pronoun *you* to speak to a pet or to the President.

What are *you* chewing on, you silly dog?
Mr. President, are *you* concerned about acid rain?

There is no difference between *you* in the singular and *you* in the plural. For example, if there were a dozen persons in a room and you asked, "Are *you* coming?" the *you* could refer to one person or to many.

IN GERMAN

There are two sets of pronouns for *you*: the familiar and formal forms.

1. The **familiar form** is used with members of one's family, friends, children, and pets. In general, you use the familiar forms with persons you call by a first name. There is a singular and a plural form.

   du → familiar singular *you*. It addresses one person.

   > Inge, bist **du** jetzt endlich fertig?
   > *Inge, are **you** finished now?*

   > Hans, was machst **du**?
   > *Hans, what are **you** doing?*

   ihr → familiar plural *you*. It addresses more than one person to whom you say **du** individually.

   > Maria und Inge, was macht **ihr**?
   > *Maria and Inge, what are **you** doing?*

   > Hans und Peter, kommt **ihr** mit?
   > *Hans and Peter, are **you** coming along?*

2. The **formal form** is used to address one or more persons you do not know very well. There is only one form.

   Sie → formal singular and plural *you*. It addresses one or more persons.

   > Herr Braun, kommen **Sie** mit?
   > *Mr. Braun, are **you** coming along?*

   > Herr und Frau Braun, kommen **Sie** mit?
   > *Mr. and Mrs. Braun, are **you** coming along?*

If you are uncertain which form of *you* to use, use the formal form, unless you are speaking to a child or an animal.

"It"—er, sie, or es?

IN ENGLISH

Whenever you refer to one thing or idea, you use the pronoun *it*.

> Where is the pencil? *It* is lying on the table.
> How was the trip? *It* was nice.

IN GERMAN

The singular pronoun you use depends on the gender of the noun *it* replaces, its antecedent (see **What is Meant by Gender?**, p. 6). Thus *it* can be either masculine, feminine, or neuter.

To choose the correct form of *it,* you must identify two things:

1. ANTECEDENT—Find the noun *it* replaces.
2. GENDER—Determine the gender of the antecedent in German.

Here is an example for each gender:

- masculine antecedent → **er**

   Where is the pencil? It is lying on the table.

   ANTECEDENT: the pencil
   GENDER: **Der Bleistift** *(pencil)* is masculine.

   Wo ist der Bleistift? **Er** liegt auf dem Tisch.
   masculine singular
   subject pronoun → nominative

- feminine antecedent → **sie**

   How was the trip? It was nice.

   ANTECEDENT: the trip
   GENDER: **Die Reise** *(trip)* is feminine.

   Wie war die Reise? **Sie** war sehr schön.
   feminine singular
   subject pronoun → nominative

- neuter antecedent → **es**

   Where is the book? It is on the table.

   ANTECEDENT: the book
   GENDER: **Das Buch** *(book)* is neuter.

   Wo ist das Buch? **Es** ist auf dem Tisch.
   neuter singular
   subject pronoun → nominative

Personal Pronouns as Objects

In the following examples a personal pronoun is used as an object of a verb (see **What are Objects?**, p. 26).

   She saw *us.*

   She saw whom? Us.
   Us is the direct object of *saw.*

   They wrote *me.*

   They wrote to whom? Me.
   Me is the indirect object of *wrote.*

IN ENGLISH

Most pronouns that occur as objects in a sentence are different in form from the ones used as subjects. When pronouns are used as the direct object, indirect object, or object of a preposition in English they are said to be in the **objective case.**

They invited *him* and *me*.　　[*He* and *I* work for the newspaper.]

direct objects　　　　　　subjects
objective case　　　　　　nominative case

I lent *them* my car.

indirect object
objective case

They are coming with *you* and *her*.

objects of a preposition
objective case

Compare the nominative and objective cases of English pronouns:

	Nominative	Objective
Singular		
1st person	I	me
2nd person	you	you
3rd person	he / she / it	him / her / it
Plural		
1st person	we	us
2nd person	you	you
3rd person	they	them

The form of the object pronoun is the same regardless of whether the pronoun is used as a direct object, an indirect object, or an object of a preposition.

IN GERMAN

Instead of a single objective case, two cases are used for pronouns that are direct objects, indirect objects, or objects of a preposition: the accusative and the dative. (A few prepositions take the genitive case, but this rarely occurs with personal pronouns.) The chart below lists each English objective pronoun and the two corresponding forms, accusative and dative, in German.

ENGLISH		GERMAN		
Objective		**Accusative**	**Dative**	
Singular				
me	1st person	**mich**	**mir**	
you	2nd person	{ **dich**	**dir**	familiar
		Sie	**Ihnen**	formal
him		{ **ihn**	**ihm**	masculine
her	3rd person	{ **sie**	**ihr**	feminine
it		{ **es**	**ihm**	neuter
Plural				
us	1st person	**uns**	**uns**	
you	2nd person	{ **euch**	**euch**	familiar
		Sie	**Ihnen**	formal
them	3rd person	**sie**	**ihnen**	

In general, once you have learned the functions of the German cases for nouns, you will have no difficulty knowing the case of pronouns, since the cases are the same. Two English object pronouns, however, have more than one equivalent in German: *you* and *it*. Let us look more closely at these object pronouns so that you can learn how to choose the correct form.

"You"—The Familiar and Formal Forms

The **familiar forms** (**du** → nominative singular; **ihr** → nominative plural) have accusative and dative forms.

- **dich** → accusative singular; **dir** → dative singular

> *We see you, Anna.*
> Wir sehen **dich**, Anna.
> |
> familiar singular
> direct object → accusative

> *We are helping you, Anna.*
> Wir helfen **dir**, Anna.
> |
> familiar singular
> dative object of **helfen** *(to help)*

- **euch** → accusative plural; **euch** → dative plural

> *We see you, Effi and Franz.*
> Wir sehen **euch**, Effi und Franz.
> |
> familiar plural
> direct object → accusative

We are helping you, Effi and Franz.
Wir helfen **euch**, Effi und Franz.
      |
      familiar plural
      dative object of **helfen** *(to help)*

The **formal form** (**Sie** → nominative) has an accusative and a dative form. The same form is used when addressing one or more persons.

- **Sie** → accusative singular and plural; **Ihnen** → dative singular and plural

We will see you tomorrow, Mrs. Erb.
Wir sehen **Sie** morgen, Frau Erb.
      |
      formal
      direct object → accusative

Prof. and Mrs. Mayer, we will certainly call you.
Prof. und Frau Mayer, wir rufen **Sie** bestimmt an.
      |
      formal
      direct object → accusative

We're glad to help you, Dr. Fried.
Wir helfen **Ihnen** gern, Dr. Fried.
      |
      formal
      dative object of **helfen** *(to help)*

"It"—ihn, ihm; sie, ihr; or es, ihm?

The German equivalent for the English pronoun *it* used as an object has six forms: masculine, feminine, and neuter, each with an accusative and dative form. You will have to determine the gender of the noun that the pronoun *it* replaces and the function of *it* in the sentence. To choose the correct form, follow these steps:

1. ANTECEDENT—Find the noun *it* replaces.
2. GENDER—Determine the gender of the antecedent in German.
3. FUNCTION—Determine the function of *it* in the sentence.
4. CASE—Choose the case that corresponds to the function.
5. SELECTION—Select the form depending on the gender and case.

Let us look at some examples.

- masculine antecedent → **ihn** (accusative); **ihm** (dative)

Did you see the film? Yes, I saw it.
    ANTECEDENT: the film
    GENDER: **Der Film** *(the film)* is masculine.

FUNCTION: direct object of *see* (**sehen**)
CASE: accusative
SELECTION: **ihn**

Hast du den Film gesehen? Ja, ich habe **ihn** gesehen.

    masculine   masculine singular
    singular   accusative object

■ feminine antecedent → **sie** (accusative); **ihr** (dative)

Are you reading the newspaper? Yes, I am reading it.

ANTECEDENT: the newspaper
GENDER: **Die Zeitung** *(the newspaper)* is feminine.
FUNCTION: direct object of *read* (**lesen**)
CASE: accusative
SELECTION: **sie**

Lesen Sie die Zeitung? Ja, ich lese **sie**.

    feminine   feminine singular
    singular   accusative object

■ neuter antecedent → **es** (accusative), **ihm** (dative)

Do you understand the book? Yes, I understand it.

ANTECEDENT: the book
GENDER: **Das Buch** is neuter.
FUNCTION: direct object of *understand* (*verstehen*)
CASE: accusative
SELECTION: **es**

Verstehen Sie das Buch? Ja, ich verstehe **es**.

    neuter   neuter singular
    singular   accusative object

Careful

Since the pronoun depends on the gender of the German noun replaced, you will also use **es** and **ihm** when you replace neuter nouns that refer to people. (In English you use *him* or *her* to refer to people.)

*Who helps the child? We are helping **her** (**him**).*

ANTECEDENT: the child
GENDER: **Das Kind** is neuter.
FUNCTION: object of *help* (**helfen** takes a dative object)
CASE: dative
SELECTION: **ihm**

Wer hilft dem Kind? Wir helfen **ihm**.

    neuter   neuter singular
    singular   dative object

Remember, too, that the German equivalents of *him* and *her* have two forms: accusative and dative. To choose the proper form, you will have to determine the function of the pronoun in the sentence.

> *Did you see the man? Yes, I saw **him**.*
>   FUNCTION: direct object of *see* (**sehen**)
>   CASE: accusative
> Hast du den Mann gesehen? Ja, ich habe **ihn** gesehn.
>   masculine singular
>   accusative object

> *Who helps the man? We are helping **him**.*
>   FUNCTION: object of *help* (**helfen** requires a dative object)
>   CASE: dative
> Wer hilft dem Mann? Wir helfen **ihm**.
>   masculine singular
>   dative object

> *Do you see the woman? Yes, I see **her**.*
>   FUNCTION: direct object of *see* (**sehen**)
>   CASE: accusative
> Hast du die Frau gesehen? Ja, ich habe **sie** gesehen.
>   feminine singular
>   accusative object

> *Who helps the woman? We are helping **her**.*
>   FUNCTION: object of *help* (**helfen** takes a dative object)
>   CASE: dative
> Wer hilft der Frau? Wir helfen **ihr**.
>   feminine singular
>   dative object

Personal Pronouns as Objects of Prepositions

IN ENGLISH

We can replace any noun object of a preposition with a pronoun object (see **What is a Preposition?**, p. 141). The pronoun can replace a person or a thing.

> John talked about *his sister*. John talked about *her*.
>   noun object of   pronoun object of
>   preposition *about*   preposition *about*

Beth talked about *her work*. Beth talked about *it*.

noun object of
preposition *about*

pronoun object of
preposition *about*

IN GERMAN

The objects of prepositions in German are in the accusative, dative, or genitive case. Normally we replace the noun object of a preposition with a pronoun object only if the noun refers to a person. A different construction is used when the pronoun refers to a thing or idea. Let us look at the two types of constructions.

"Person"

When the pronoun object of a preposition refers to a person (or an animal), you will follow the steps you have already learned to choose the appropriate personal pronoun:

1. ANTECEDENT—Find the noun replaced.
2. GENDER—Determine the gender of the antecedent in German.
3. CASE—Identify the case required by the preposition.
4. SELECTION—Select the appropriate pronoun form from the chart on p. 45.

Below are examples showing how to analyze sentences that have a pronoun referring to a person as the object of a preposition.

*Molly is buying something for **her brother**.*
Molly kauft etwas für **ihren Bruder**.

ANTECEDENT: brother
GENDER: **Der Bruder** *(brother)* is masculine.
CASE: **für** takes an accusative object
SELECTION: **ihn**

*Molly is buying something for **him**.*
Molly kauft etwas für **ihn**.

*John talked about **his sister**.*
John sprach von **seiner Schwester**.

ANTECEDENT: sister
GENDER: **Die Schwester** *(sister)* is feminine.
CASE: **von** takes a dative object
SELECTION: **ihr**

*John talked about **her**.*
John sprach von **ihr**.

"Thing"

Normally a pronoun cannot be the object of a preposition when you refer to a thing or an idea. When you encounter the English construction preposition + *it* or preposition + *them*, you will need to use a special German construction called a **da-compound** or a **pronominal adverb**. This construction takes the place of a preposition + a pronoun. It is formed by adding the prefix **da-** to the preposition (**dar-** if the preposition begins with a vowel). Let us look at some examples:

> *Don't think **about the work**.*
> Denken Sie nicht **an die Arbeit**!
>   preposition   noun (a thing)
>   object of preposition **an**

> *Don't think **about it**.*
> Denken Sie nicht **daran**!
>   **da-**construction:
>   **da + r + preposition an**

> *Beth talked **about her courses**.*
> Beth sprach **von ihren Kursen**.
>   preposition   noun (a thing)
>   object of preposition **von**

> *Beth talked **about them**.*
> Beth sprach **davon**.
>   **da-**construction:
>   **da + preposition von**

Your German textbook will discuss this construction and its use in greater detail.

▼▼▼▼▼▼▼▼▼▼▼▼▼▼▼▼▼REVIEW▼▼▼▼▼▼▼▼▼▼▼▼▼▼▼▼▼▼

I. Write the German subject pronoun that you would use to replace the words in *italics*.

                                                                          German

1. Mom, have *you* seen my jacket?   _____

2. *Cathy and I* are going out.   _____

3. Children, *you* must come inside.   _____

4. Dr. Clark, what do *you* think?   _____

II. Write the English subject pronoun in the first column.
- Using the translations given and the chart on p. 41, fill in the equivalent German nominative pronoun in the German column.

	English	**German**
1. *The window* is open. (**das Fenster**)	_____	_____
2. *The street* was deserted. (**die Straße**)	_____	_____
3. *The cake* tastes great. (**der Kuchen**)	_____	_____

III. The following English sentences contain prepositions and their objects written in italics.
- Circle italicized nouns referring to persons.
- Underline italicized nouns referring to things.
- Indicate the type of construction you must use in German: preposition + personal pronoun (PP) or **da**-compound (**da**-c).

1. We're waiting *for Greg*.	PP	DA-C
2. Thank you *for the present*!	PP	DA-C
3. I wrote *to Emily*.	PP	DA-C
4. We're looking forward *to the vacation*.	PP	DA-C

IV. Using the chart on p. 45, indicate the information requested about the pronouns in **bold**. NUMBER: singular (S) or plural (P), GENDER: masculine (M), feminine (F), or neuter (N) and CASE: nominative (N), accusative (Acc.) or dative (D) case.

1. Ich glaube **dir**.

PERSON:	1st	2nd	3rd
NUMBER:	S	P	
CASE:	N	ACC	D

2. Wir sahen **ihn** oft.

PERSON:	1st	2nd	3rd
GENDER:	M	F	N
NUMBER:	S	P	
CASE:	N	ACC	D

13. WHAT ARE THE PRINCIPAL PARTS OF A VERB?

The **principal parts** of a verb are the forms we need to create all the different tenses (see **What is Meant by Tense?**, p. 62).

IN ENGLISH

The principal parts of an English verb are the infinitive, the past tense, and the past participle (see **What is an Infinitive?**, p. 55, **What is the Past Tense?**, p. 65, and **What is a Participle?**, p. 71). If you know these parts, you can form all the other tenses of a verb.

For example, in order to form the six main tenses of the verb *to eat*, we need to know *eat* (the form used in the infinitive), *ate* (the past), and *eaten* (the past participle).

present	I eat
present perfect	I have eaten
past	I ate
past perfect	I had eaten
future	I will eat
future perfect	I will have eaten

English verbs fall into two categories depending on how they form their principal parts:

1. **Regular verbs** form their past tense and past participle predictably by simply adding *-ed*, *-d*, or *-t* to the base of the infinitive.

Infinitive	Past tense	Past participle
to walk	walk*ed*	walk*ed*
to seem	seem*ed*	seem*ed*
to burn	burn*ed* (burn*t*)	burn*ed* (burn*t*)

Since the past tense and the past participle of regular verbs are identical, these verbs have only two distinct principal parts, the infinitive and the past.

2. **Irregular verbs** have unpredictable principal parts. As we grow up, we learn these forms simply by hearing them. Examples of verbs with irregular principal parts include the following:

Infinitive	Past Tense	Past Participle
to sing	sang	sung
to draw	drew	drawn
to hit	hit	hit
to lie	lay	lain
to ride	rode	ridden

IN GERMAN

The three principal parts are essentially the same as in English: the infinitive, the past tense, and the past participle. For some verbs a fourth principal part (discussed below) is also important.

German verbs fall into two categories depending on how they form their principal parts: weak verbs and strong verbs.[1]

1. **Weak verbs** resemble English regular verbs in that they form their principal parts predictably, using the stem of the verb. The stem is the main part of the verb, the part that gives us the verb's meaning (to find the stem, see p. 60).

   - the past tense is formed by adding a **-t-** (or if the verb stem ends in **-d** or **-t**, by adding **-et-**) to the stem of the infinitive and then adding the endings for the different persons.

   - the past participle is formed by adding the prefix **ge-** and the suffix **-t** or **-et** to the stem of the verb.

Infinitive	Past Tense	Past Participle
	(3rd per. sing.)	
machen	mach**te**	**ge**mach**t**
arbeiten	arbeit**ete**	**ge**arbeit**et**
glauben	glaub**te**	**ge**glaub**t**

2. **Strong verbs,** like English irregular verbs, have unpredictable principal parts. You will simply have to memorize them as new vocabulary.

   - the vowel of the infinitive stem may change in the past tense and in the past participle.

   - the past participle ends in **-en**, or, rarely, in **-n**.

Infinitive	Past tense	Past participle
	(3rd per. sing.)	
finden	fand	**ge**fund**en**
kommen	kam	**ge**komm**en**
verlieren	verlor	verlor**en**
singen	sang	**ge**sung**en**
tun	tat	**ge**tan

   As you can see, there is no additional **-t** in either the past tense or the past participle as there is in the weak verbs.

---

[1]A small group of irregular verbs falls between these two categories. Your German textbook will show you how to form the principal parts of these verbs.

- the stem vowel in the 2nd and 3rd person singular of the present tense changes in some verbs. In these cases you will need to know a fourth principal part, i.e., the 3rd person singular of the present tense.

Infinitive	Present (3rd per. sing.)	Past tense	Past participle
laufen	er läuft	lief	gelaufen
lesen	liest	las	gelesen
schlafen	schläft	schlief	geschlafen
nehmen	nimmt	nahm	genommen

Only by memorizing the principal parts of the strong verbs can you conjugate them properly in all their tenses.

▼▼▼▼▼▼▼▼▼▼▼▼▼▼▼▼▼REVIEW▼▼▼▼▼▼▼▼▼▼▼▼▼▼▼▼▼

Examine these principal parts and indicate whether the following German verbs are weak (w) or strong (s).

1. kaufen—kaufte-(hat) gekauft   w   s

2. beginnen—begann-(hat) begonnen   w   s

3. liegen—lag-(hat) gelegen   w   s

4. fragen—fragte-(hat) gefragt   w   s

5. sitzen—saß-(hat) gesessen   w   s

14. WHAT IS AN INFINITIVE?

The **infinitive** is the form of the verb found in the dictionary as the main entry.

IN ENGLISH
The infinitive is used together with a main verb, that is a conjugated verb, to form various types of sentences (see **What is a Verb Conjugation?**, p. 57). When using an infinitive in a sentence we often combine *to* + the dictionary form of the verb, i.e., *to be, to walk, to think.*

To learn is challenging.
infinitive main verb

It is important *to be* on time.
main verb   infinitive

Bob and Mary want *to play* tennis.
               main verb infinitive

It has started *to rain.*
      main verb   infinitive

After some verbs, such as *must* and *let*, we use the dictionary form of the verb, i.e., the infinitive, without the *to.*

Jackie must *do* her homework.
      main verb   dictionary form

The parents let the children *open* the presents.
          main verb   dictionary form

IN GERMAN
The infinitive ends with the letters **-n** or **-en**. It is used in a variety of ways. There will generally be another conjugated verb with it that serves as the main verb in the sentence.

*Bob wants **to play** tennis.*
Bob will Tennis **spielen**.
conjugated verb   infinitive

*Mary doesn't have **to work**.*
Mary braucht nicht **zu arbeiten**.
　　　　|　　　　　　|_____|
　　conjugated verb　　infinitive

▼▼▼▼▼▼▼▼▼▼▼▼▼▼▼▼▼▼REVIEW▼▼▼▼▼▼▼▼▼▼▼▼▼▼▼▼▼▼▼

Write the infinitive form of the verbs in *italics* in the space provided.

1. We *taught* them everything they know.　　　＿＿＿＿＿＿＿

2. I *am* tired today.　　　＿＿＿＿＿＿＿

3. They *had* a good time.　　　＿＿＿＿＿＿＿

4. She *leaves* next week for Konstanz.　　　＿＿＿＿＿＿＿

5. He *swam* every day in the summer.　　　＿＿＿＿＿＿＿

15. WHAT IS A VERB CONJUGATION?

A **verb conjugation** is a list of the six possible forms of the verb for a particular tense. For each tense, there is one verb form for each of the six persons used as the subject of the verb.

IN ENGLISH

Most verbs change very little. Let us look at the forms of the verb *to sing* in the present tense when each of the six possible pronouns is the subject (see **What is a Personal Pronoun?**, p. 40).[1]

Singular

1st person	*I sing* with the music.
2nd person	*You sing* with the music.
3rd person	⎧ *He sings* with the music. ⎨ *She sings* with the music. ⎩ *It sings* with the music.

Plural

1st person	*We sing* with the music.
2nd person	*You sing* with the music.
3rd person	*They sing* with the music.

English verbs change so little, that you do not need to "conjugate verbs." It is much simpler to remember that verbs add an "**-s**" in the 3rd person singular.

IN GERMAN

German verbs have many more forms than English verbs. Fortunately, the conjugations are quite predictable for most verbs, once you have learned a few simple rules.

Verb Subjects

Let us look at the same verb *to sing* in German (**singen**), paying special attention to the personal subject pronoun.

Singular

1st person	**ich** singe
2nd person familiar	**du** singst
3rd person	⎧ **er** singt ⎨ **sie** singt ⎩ **es** singt

---

[1] In this section we will talk only about the present tense (see **What is the Present Tense?**, p. 63).

Plural

1st person	**wir** singen
2nd person familiar	**ihr** singt
2nd person formal	**Sie** singen
(singular & plural)	
3rd person	**sie** singen

1st person singular—The "*I* form" of the verb (the **ich** form) is used whenever the person speaking is the doer of the action.

> **Ich singe** leise.
> *I sing softly.*

2nd person singular—The "*you* familiar singular form" of the verb (the **du** form) is used whenever the person spoken to (with whom you are on familiar terms, see p. 42) is the doer of the action.

> Molly, **du singst** gut.
> *Molly, you sing well.*

3rd person singular—The "3rd person singular form" of the verb (the **er, sie, es** form) is used when the person, thing, or idea spoken about is the doer of the action. The 3rd person singular form is used with:

- the third person singular masculine pronoun **er** *(he or it)*, feminine pronoun **sie** *(she or it)*, and the neuter pronoun **es** *(it)*

> **Er singt** schön.
> *He sings beautifully.*
>
> **Sie singt** schön.
> *She sings beautifully.*
>
> **Es singt** schön.
> *It sings beautifully.*

- one proper name

> Anna **singt** gut.
> *Anna sings well.*

- a singular noun

> Der Vogel **singt**.
> *The bird sings.*
>
> Die Geige **singt**.
> *The violin sings.*
>
> Das Kind **singt**.
> *The child sings.*

1st person plural—The *"we* form of the verb" (the **wir** form) is used whenever *I* (the speaker) is one of the doers of the action; that is, whenever the speaker is included in a plural or multiple subject.

Peter, Paul, Mary und ich **singen** gut.
|_____| |
     subjects + **ich**   **wir** form

Peter, Paul, Mary and I sing well.
|_____| |
     subjects + *I*   *we* form

In this sentence, the subject, *Peter, Paul, Mary and I*, could be replaced by the pronoun *we*; thus in German you must use the **wir** form (lst person plural) of the verb.

2nd person plural—The *"you* plural familiar form" of the verb (the **ihr** form) is used whenever you are addressing more than one person to whom you say **du** individually.

Molly, **singst du** auch?   Win, **singst du** auch?
Molly, do you sing too?   *Win, do you sing too?*

Molly und Win, **ihr singt** auch?
Molly and Win, do you sing too?

2nd person formal, singular and plural—The "formal *you* form" of the verb (the **Sie** form), singular and plural, is used whenever you are addressing one or more persons to whom you say **Sie**.

Frau Smith, **kommen Sie** mit?
Mrs. Smith, are you coming along with us?

Herr und Frau Smith, **kommen Sie** mit?
Mr. and Mrs. Smith, are you coming along with us?

3rd person plural—The *"they* form" of the verb (the **sie** form) is used whenever you are speaking about two or more persons or things that do not include either the speaker or the person spoken to.

Die Kinder **singen** im Chor.
     In German: **sie** form
The children sing in the choir.

Paul und Mary **singen** ein Duett.   [Compare: Paul, Mary, and I *sing*.]
     In German: **sie** form   In German: **wir** form
Paul and Mary sing a duet.

Die Gläser und Teller **sind** auf dem Tisch.

In German: **sie** form

*The glasses and plates **are** on the table.*

In the three sentences above, the subject could be replaced by the pronoun *they*; thus in German you must use the **sie** form, the 3rd person plural of the verb.

Verb Forms

Let us look again at the verb *to sing* (**singen**) conjugated in the present tense, paying special attention to its different forms.

ich	sing**e**	wir	sing**en**
du	sing**st**	ihr	sing**t**
er	sing**t**	sie	sing**en**
sie	sing**t**	Sie	sing**en**
es	sing**t**		

A German verb is composed of two parts:

1. **the stem**, obtained by dropping the final **-en** from the infinitive (or with a few verbs like **tun** and **ändern** by dropping the final **-n**)

Infinitive	Stem
singen	sing-
machen	mach-
kommen	komm-

2. **the personal endings**, which change for each person, with some overlap.

As you can see in the verb **singen** conjugated above, the endings for the present tense are **-e, -st, -t, -en, -t, -en**.

To use a verb correctly in a sentence, follow these two steps.

1. Sᴛᴇᴍ—Find the verb stem by removing the infinitive ending.

brauch**en**   brauch-

infinitive   stem
ending

2. Eɴᴅɪɴɢ—Add the ending that agrees with the subject.

Ich **brauche** Hilfe.

verb stem **brauch-** + ending **-e**

*I **need** help.*

subject *I* → **ich** form

Wir **brauchen** auch Hilfe.
verb stem **brauch-** + ending **-en**
*We **need** help too.*
subject *we* → **wir** form

Some verb stems require slight adjustments in the endings. In addition, many of the so-called strong verbs change their stem in the 2nd
and 3rd person singular form (see p. 54) of the present tense. Finally,
a very few German verbs are irregular in the present tense, that is,
they do not follow a predictable pattern. Your German textbook will
give you the conjugations of these irregular verbs.

▼▼▼▼▼▼▼▼▼▼▼▼▼▼▼▼▼▼REVIEW▼▼▼▼▼▼▼▼▼▼▼▼▼▼▼▼▼▼

I. Draw a box around the stem of the German verbs in the infinitive form.

1. denken

2. rennen

3. arbeiten

4. wandern

5. reisen

II. Using the chart of p. 60, conjugate the verb **gehen** *(to go)*.

STEM: _____

ich   _____

du   _____

er, sie, es _____

wir   _____

ihr   _____

sie, Sie   _____

16. WHAT IS MEANT BY TENSE?

The **tense** of a verb indicates the time when the action expressed by the verb takes place: at the present time, in the past, or in the future.

present	I am eating
past	I ate
future	I will eat

As you can see in the above examples, just by putting the verb in a different tense and without giving any additional information (such as "I am eating *now*," "I ate *yesterday*," "I will eat *tomorrow*"), you can indicate when the action of the verb takes, took, or will take place. There are six main tenses in English: present, present perfect, past, past perfect, future, and future perfect. This handbook discusses each of these tenses in separate sections.

17. WHAT IS THE PRESENT TENSE?

The **present tense** indicates that the action is happening at the present time. It can be:

- when the speaker is speaking   I *see* you.
- a habitual action   He *smokes* when he *is* nervous.
- a general truth   The sun *shines* every day.

IN ENGLISH
There are three forms of the verb which, although they have slightly different meanings, all indicate the present tense.

> **present**   Mary *studies* in the library.
> **present progressive**   Mary *is studying* in the library.
> **present emphatic**   Mary *does study* in the library.

In conversation, you automatically choose one of these three present tense forms depending on what you want to say.

> Where does Mary study?
> She *studies* in the library.

> Where is Mary studying now?
> She *is studying* in the library.

> Does Mary really study in the library?
> Yes, she really *does study* in the library.

IN GERMAN
There is only one verb form to indicate the present tense. This single form corresponds to the English present, present progressive, and present emphatic tenses. In German the present tense is indicated by the ending of the verb, without any helping or auxiliary verb such as *is* or *does* (see **What are Auxiliary Verbs?**, p. 67).

> Mary *studies* at the university.
> studiert

> Mary *is studying* at the university.
> studiert

> Mary *does study* at the university.
> studiert

Your German textbook will explain how to form this tense.

▼▼▼▼▼▼▼▼▼▼▼▼▼▼▼▼▼▼REVIEW▼▼▼▼▼▼▼▼▼▼▼▼▼▼▼▼▼▼

Circle the words that correspond to the German present tense.

- Using the chart on p. 60, fill in the forms of the verb **spielen** *(to play)* that agree with the pronoun subjects given.

1. So John and Vera really do play tennis.   (pl.) sie _____

2. Yes, John plays often.   er   _____

3. In fact, Vera is playing right now too.   sie   _____

4. Our friends are playing with them.   (pl.) sie _____

5. Do you play too?   du   _____

18. WHAT IS THE PAST TENSE?

The **past tense** is used to express an action that occurred in the past.

IN ENGLISH
There are several verb forms that indicate that an action took place in the past.

simple past (*or* past)	I worked
past progressive	I was working
past emphatic	I did work

The simple past is called a **simple tense** because it consists of only one word. The past progressive and the past emphatic are called **compound tenses** because they consist of more than one word.

English also has three other compound tenses for expressing past actions. These are the perfect tenses.

present perfect	I have worked
past perfect	I had worked

These last two tenses will be discussed together with the future perfect in a separate section (see **What are the Perfect Tenses?**, p. 79).

IN GERMAN
The two German tenses for expressing an action in the past are the simple past and the perfect.

1. The **simple past** consists of only one word. This tense is also called the imperfect (**Imperfekt**) or the preterite (**Präteritum**).

2. The **perfect** tense (**Perfekt**) is a compound tense, consisting of two parts.

The formation of both the simple past and the perfect depends on whether the verb is a so-called strong verb or a weak verb (see p. 53). Your German textbook will explain in detail the formation of these two tenses for both groups of verbs.

It is important to remember that these two tenses have equivalent meanings. Their difference is one of style: generally, the perfect is used for a conversational style, and the simple past is used for narration.

▼▼▼▼▼▼▼▼▼▼▼▼▼▼▼▼▼▼▼REVIEW▼▼▼▼▼▼▼▼▼▼▼▼▼▼▼▼▼▼▼

I. For each of the following verbs, fill in the three English past tense verb forms.

1. to write   I _____

                l _____

                I _____

2. to laugh   she _____

                she _____

                she _____

II. Below are pairs of sentences in German in the simple past and perfect tenses. Write the simple past form in English. It is the translation that would usually be the best equivalent for these German verb tenses.

1. Sie sprachen.   They _____

   Sie haben gesprochen.

   (**sprechen** → *to speak*)

2. Es regnete.   It   _____

   Es hat geregnet.

   (**regnen** → *to rain*)

3. Er telephonierte.   He   _____

   Er hat telephoniert.

   (**telephonieren** → *to telephone*)

19. WHAT ARE AUXILIARY VERBS?

A verb is called an **auxiliary verb** or **helping verb** when it helps another verb, called a **main verb**, form one of its tenses (see **What is Meant by Tense?**, p. 62). When it is used alone, it functions as a main verb.

Kit *is* a girl.	*is*	**main verb**
Tom *has* a headache.	*has*	**main verb**
They *go* to the movies.	*go*	**main verb**
They ***have** gone* to the movies.	***have***	**auxiliary verb**

       complete verb   *gone*   **past participle of main verb**

She ***has been** gone* for three hours.

       complete verb

	has	**auxiliary verb**
	been	**auxiliary verb**
	gone	**past participle of main verb**

IN ENGLISH

There are many auxiliary verbs, for example, *to have, to be*, and *to do*. They have three main uses:

- to indicate the tense of the sentence (present, past and future)

present	Liz *is reading* a book.
past	Liz *was reading* a book.
future	Liz *will read* a book.

- to help formulate questions

Bob *has* a dog.	*has*	**main verb**
Does Bob *have* a dog?	*does*	**auxiliary verb**
	have	**main verb**

- to indicate the passive voice (see **What is Meant by Active and Passive Voice?**, p. 150)

    The book *is read* by many people.

IN GERMAN

The three main auxiliary verbs are **haben** *(to have)*, **sein** *(to be)*, and **werden** *(to become)*.

- **haben** and **sein** are used as auxiliaries to form the perfect tenses of verbs. Some verbs use **haben** and some use **sein** (see **What are the Perfect Tenses?**, p. 79).

Die Frau **hat** ihre Zeitung **gefunden**.

      auxiliary verb   past participle of **finden**

      hat gefunden → present perfect

*The woman **has found** her newspaper.*
*The woman **found** her newspaper.*

Der Student **ist** sehr spät **gekommen**.

      auxiliary verb   past participle of **kommen**

      ist gekommen → present perfect

*The student **has come** very late.*
*The student **came** very late.*

- **werden** is used to form the future tenses and the passive voice (see **What is the Future Tense?**, p. 83)

Sie **werden zahlen**.

     auxiliary verb infinitive

     werden zahlen → future tense

*They **will pay**.*

Das Haus **wird** jetzt **gebaut**.

      auxiliary verb   past participle of **bauen**

      wird gebaut → passive voice, present tense

*The house **is** now **being built**.*

Use of Auxiliaries in English and in German

You will find that German and English often do not overlap in their use of auxiliaries. Equivalents for the English auxiliary verbs *do, does,* and *did* do not exist in German. When you encounter them in an English sentence which you are trying to express in German, use them as a guide to tense, but do not translate them.

Do they live here?

    auxiliary   main verb
    verb
    present tense verb

Wohnen sie hier?

    main verb
    wohnen *(to live)*
    present tense

English often uses forms of the verb *to be* *(is, was, will be)* as an auxiliary verb with a present participle (see **What is a Participle?**, p. 71). When you encounter this construction in an English sentence you are going to express in German, use the auxiliary verb as a guide to tense and put the main verb in the appropriate German tense.

*We **are working** today.*
    | |
auxiliary main verb
verb   present participle
present

Wir **arbeiten** heute.
       |
       main verb
       arbeiten *(work)*
       present

Modal Auxiliaries

IN ENGLISH
There is a group of auxiliary verbs called **modal auxiliaries**. The word *modal* is related to *mode,* which means the manner of doing something. These modal verbs (e.g., *can, may, should, must*) show the attitude of the speaker toward what he or she is saying, while the main verb indicates an action. In all the sentences below, the action expressed by the main verb *(read)* is not actually occurring; it is being discussed.

Chris *can* read this book.

  [Chris *has the ability to* read the book.]

Chris *may* read this book.

  [Chris *is allowed to* read the book.]

Chris *must* read this book.

  [Chris *has to* read the book.]

Chris *should* read this book.

  [Chris *ought to* read the book.]

IN GERMAN
German also has a group of auxiliary verbs called modal auxiliaries: **können** *(to be able, can),* **sollen** *(to be supposed to, should),* **müssen** *(to be obligated to, must),* **dürfen** *(to be permitted to, may),* **wollen** *(to want to),* and **mögen** *(to like to).* (The verb **lassen**, *to let, to allow,*

is sometimes grouped with model auxiliaries.) Modal auxiliaries are usually used with the infinitive of another verb.

Inge **will mitkommen**.
modal auxiliary   infinitive
present tense

*Inge **wants to come** along.*

Der Zug **sollte** pünktlich **ankommen**.
modal auxiliary   infinitive
past tense

*The train **was supposed to arrive** on time.*

When you learn the modal verbs in German, especially **wollen** and **mögen**, you will need to pay careful attention to their definitions because they are not always equivalent in meaning to English modal verbs. Your textbook will explain the meanings of the German modal verbs and give you examples of how they are used.

▼▼▼▼▼▼▼▼▼▼▼▼▼▼▼▼REVIEW▼▼▼▼▼▼▼▼▼▼▼▼▼▼▼▼

I. Circle the auxiliary verbs in the following English sentences.

1. They are working on the problem.

2. We can go now.

3. You do have a point.

4. She has been waiting a long time.

5. He will arrive later.

II. Underline the English auxiliary verbs that will not be expressed by auxiliary verbs in German.
- Circle the English verb that will be expressed as the main verb of the German sentence.

1. The circus is coming to town.

2. Paul always reads the newspaper.

3. Maria drives too fast.

4. We are packing our bags.

5. Does Meg have everything?

20. WHAT IS A PARTICIPLE?

A **participle** has two functions:

1. It is a form of the verb that is used in combination with an auxiliary verb to create certain tenses.

> I was *writing* a letter.
> | |
> auxiliary participle

2. It may be used as an adjective or modifier to describe something.

> The *broken* vase was on the floor.
> |
> participle describing *vase*

There are two types of participles: the **present participle** and the **past participle**. As you will see, participles are not used in the same way in English and German.

Present Participle

IN ENGLISH

The present participle is easy to recognize because it ends in *-ing*: *working, studying, dancing, playing*, etc.

The present participle has various functions:

- as a verb—the present participle, with the auxiliary verb *to be*, can form compound tenses

> She *is singing*.
> |
> present auxiliary + present participle → present progressive

> They *were dancing*.
> |
> past auxiliary + present participle → past progressive

- as an adjective—the present participle can be an attributive adjectives (see p. 124)

> This is an *amazing* discovery.
> |
> describes the noun *discovery*

> Elise read an *interesting* book.
> |
> describes the noun *book*

- in a phrase—the present participle can begin a participial phrases (see p. 160)

> *Turning the corner*, Tony ran into a tree.
>
> The phrase *turning the corner* describes *Tony*.

> Look at the cat *climbing the tree*.
>
> The phrase *climbing the tree* describes *cat*.

IN GERMAN

The present participle is formed by adding **-d** to the infinitive.

Infinitive	Present Participle
singen	singen**d**
spielen	spielen**d**
sprechen	sprechen**d**

The present participle occurs less frequently than in English and it is not used in the same way. Never assume that an English word ending with *-ing* is translated by its German counterpart ending in **-d**.

The present participle has various functions:

- as an adjective—Like English, German often uses the present participle as an attributive adjective.

> die **singenden** Kinder
> *the singing children*

> ein **spielendes** Mädchen
> *a playing girl*

In such usage, the participle functions as any other attributive adjective and takes adjective endings. Look at **What is an Adjective?**, p. 123, for additional help and examples.

- in an extended adjectival construction—To modify nouns, formal German can use present participles in a group of words called an **extended adjectival construction**. This construction is similar to the participial phrase in English insofar as both structures use participles together with other words to give us information about a noun. An extended adjectival construction is generally placed before the noun it modifies and after the article, if there is one. In this construction, the present participle functions as an attributive adjective and takes the adjective endings.

Singing loudly in the garden, *the child played all morning.*

        participial phrase   article + noun

The participial phrase modifies the noun *child*.

Das **laut in dem Garten singende** Kind spielte den ganzen Morgen.

article   noun

                             adjective ending **-e**

extended adjectival construction
"loudly in the garden singing"

The extended adjectival construction modifies **Kind** *(child)*.

Careful

As a beginner, you must keep in mind that the equivalents of English tenses formed with an auxiliary + present participle *(she is singing, they were dancing)* do not use participles in German. English constructions using participles simply correspond to particular German tenses of the verb, and these are often expressed with a single word.

She is singing.
Sie **singt**.
    present

They were dancing.
Sie **tanzten**.
    simple past

He will be writing.
Er **wird schreiben**.
        future

Present Participle Versus Gerund

An English verb ending in *-ing* is not always a present participle; it can be a verbal noun. A **verbal noun**, also called a **gerund,** is the form of a verb which functions as a noun in a sentence. Since German verbal nouns differ in form from present participles, we will discuss them here so that you can learn to recognize them.

IN ENGLISH

A gerund ends in **-ing** and can function in a sentence in almost any way that a noun can. It can be a subject, a direct object, an indirect object, and an object of a preposition.

- a word ending in *-ing* is a gerund if you can form a question by replacing that word with the interrogative *what*. The gerund will answer this one-word question.

> *Reading* can be fun.
> |
> noun from the verb *to read*
> subject of the sentence
> > What can be fun? Reading.

> We have often thought about *moving* away.
> |
> > noun from the verb *to move*
> > object of preposition *about*
> > We often thought about what? Moving.

- a word ending in *-ing* is a present participle if you must form a question by replacing that word with more than one word or the verb *to do*.

> We are *singing*.
> |
> present participle
> > What are we doing? Singing.

IN GERMAN

Verbal nouns are usually expressed by a neuter noun made from the infinitive of the verb.

lesen	*to read*	→	das Lesen	*reading*
singen	*to sing*	→	das Singen	*singing*

You can recognize verbal nouns by identifying their function in a sentence. Since all German nouns are capitalized, you should be able to spot verbal nouns easily.

> Wir **reden** viel.
> |
> verb
> *We **are talking** a lot.*

> **Reden** ist Silber, **Schweigen** ist Gold.
> | | | |
> verbal verb   verbal verb
> noun   noun
> ***Talking** is silver, **being silent** is gold.*
> [Proverb: "Silence is golden."]

Past Participle

IN ENGLISH

This is the verb form you would use following *I have*: *I have talked, I have reached, I have taught.*

The "regular" verbs form their past participle by adding *-ed*, *-d*, or *-t* to the infinitive or dictionary form of the verb.

Infinitive	Past participle
help	help*ed*
walk	walk*ed*
burn	burn*ed* or burn*t*

The "irregular" verbs form their past participle by changing their stem vowel (see p. 52) or by making other changes. Many of the most common English verbs are irregular.

Infinitive	Past participle
go	gone
ride	ridden
speak	spoken

Notice that often, though not always, the past participle of irregular English verbs ends in "-n."

The past participle has various functions:

- as a verb form—the past participle, with the auxiliary verb *to have*, can form compound tenses, or with the auxiliary verb *to be*, can form the passive voice

    I <u>*have written*</u> all that I have to say.

    auxiliary *to have* + past participle → compound tense

    Truer words <u>*were* never *spoken*</u>.

    auxiliary *to be* + participle →passive voice

- as an adjective—the past participle can be an attributive adjective

    Is the *written* word more important than the *spoken* word?
    describes the noun *word*   describes the noun *word*

- in a phrase—the past participle can begin a participial phrase

    We didn't notice the sign *posted on the door.*

    The phrase *posted on the door* describes the noun *sign.*

IN GERMAN

Past participles are formed differently depending on whether a verb is weak or strong (see p. 53): weak verbs form their past participle according to a regular rule; strong verbs have irregular past participles. For both groups, however, the **ge-** prefix most commonly characterizes the past participle (see **What are Prefixes and Suffixes?**, p. 146).

WEAK VERBS—The past participles of weak verbs are formed by adding a prefix and a suffix.

- **ge-** is added to the front of the stem (unless the verb begins with an inseparable prefix). Because **ge-** is placed before the stem, it is called a **prefix**.
- **-t** is added to the end of the stem. Because **-t** is placed after the stem, it is called a **suffix**.

Infinitive	Stem	Past participle	
machen	mach-	**ge**mach**t**	*made*
glauben	glaub-	**ge**glaub**t**	*believed*

Some verb stems require slight adjustments. There are special rules for forming the past participle of verbs that already begin with prefixes and for verbs that end with the suffix **-ieren**. Your German textbook will explain how to handle these verbs.

STRONG VERBS—The past participles of strong verbs often change the vowel in the stem, and occasionally some of the consonants. As with weak verbs, there are special rules for forming the past participle of strong verbs that already begin with a prefix. Here are some characteristics common to past participles of strong verbs.

- **ge-** is added to the front of the stem (unless the verb already begins with an inseparable prefix)
- the ending is **-en** (or, rarely, **-n**)

Infinitive	Past participle	
schlafen	**ge**schlaf**en**	*slept*
gehen	**ge**gang**en**	*gone*
finden	**ge**fund**en**	*found*
liegen	**ge**leg**en**	*lain*

Since there is no way to predict the past participle of a strong verb, you will have to memorize it when the verb is presented. Remember that the past participle of strong verbs always ends in **-en** (or **-n**), while the past participle of weak verbs always ends in **-t**.

Like English, German uses the past participle to form verb tenses, the passive voice, and attributive adjectives:

- as a verb form—The most important use of the past participle in German is in verb combinations: all the perfect tenses are formed with an auxiliary verb, either **haben** *(to have)* or **sein** *(to be)* + the past participle. Look at **What are the Perfect Tenses?**, p. 79, for information on this use of the past participle.

  The passive voice is formed with the auxiliary verb **werden** *(to become)* + the past participle. Look at **What is Meant by Active and Passive Voice?**, p. 150, to learn more about this usage.

- as an adjective—the past participle can be used as an attributive adjective. In this usage, the rules about endings are the same as for any other attributive adjective. Look at **What is a Descriptive Adjective?**, p. 124, for help in choosing the proper adjective ending.

  Ich verstehe **die gesprochene Sprache** nicht.
  I do not understand the spoken language.

  Die eingeladenen Gäste sind alle gekommen.
  The invited guests all came.

- in an extended adjectival construction—To modify nouns, formal German can use past participles in a group of words as part of an extended adjectival construction. The extended adjectival construction is similar to the participial phrase in English insofar as both structures use participles together with other words to give us information about the nouns they describe. An extended adjectival construction with a past participle is generally placed before the noun it modifies and after the article, if there is one. When this occurs, the past participle functions as an attributive adjective and takes the adjective endings.

  *She sat down on the bench **screwed to the wall**.*

  article + noun   participial phrase

  The participial phrase modifies the noun *bench*.

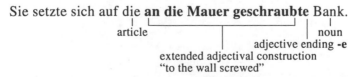

  Sie setzte sich auf die **an die Mauer geschraubte** Bank.

  article   noun
                                                      adjective ending -e
                       extended adjectival construction
                       "to the wall screwed"

  The extended adjectival construction modifies **Bank** *(bench).*

▼▼▼▼▼▼▼▼▼▼▼▼▼▼▼▼▼▼REVIEW▼▼▼▼▼▼▼▼▼▼▼▼▼▼▼▼▼▼

I. Circle the participles in the following sentences.
- Indicate whether each participle is a present (P) or past participle (PP).

1. They are working late.   P   PP

2. Don't cry over spilled milk.   P   PP

3. Falling prices hurt farmers last month.   P   PP

4. The treasure from the sunken ship was priceless.   P   PP

5. It was a heated debate.   P   PP

II. Indicate whether the *-ing* word in the following sentences is a present
   participle (P) or gerund (G).

1. We are coming tomorrow.   P   G

2. Littering is prohibited.   P   G

3. This is a good place for sunbathing.   P   G

4. The leaves are turning red.   P   G

21. WHAT ARE THE PERFECT TENSES?

The **perfect tenses** are compound tenses of the verb made up of an auxiliary verb + the past participle (see **What are Auxiliary Verbs?**, p. 67, and p. 75 in **What is a Participle?**). We use the perfect tenses to express actions that took place in the past or to indicate the sequence of events.

I *have* not *seen* him.
auxiliary   past participle of *to see*
verb
present of *to have*

They *were* already *gone*.
    auxiliary   past participle of *to go*
    verb
    past of *to be*

As you can see, the auxiliary verb can be put in different tenses.

IN ENGLISH

There are three perfect tenses formed with the auxiliary verb *to have* + the past participle of the main verb. The name of each perfect tense is based on the tense of the auxiliary verb.

PRESENT PERFECT—*to have* in the present tense + the past participle of the main verb.

I *have eaten*.
auxiliary past participle
verb   of *to eat*

They *have washed* the car.
    auxiliary past participle
    verb   of *to wash*

PAST PERFECT (pluperfect)—*to have* in the simple past tense + the past participle of the main verb.

I *had eaten* before 6:00 o'clock.
auxiliary past participle
verb   of *to eat*

They *had washed* the car before the storm.
    auxiliary past participle
    verb   of *to wash*

FUTURE PERFECT—*to have* in the future tense + the past participle of the main verb.

I *shall have eaten* by 6:00.

    auxiliary past participle
    verbs   of *to eat*

They *will have washed* the car by Thursday.

        auxiliary past participle
        verbs   of *to wash*

IN GERMAN

As in English there are three perfect tenses; they are the present perfect (**Perfekt**), the past perfect or pluperfect (**Plusquamperfekt**), and the future perfect, which occurs infrequently. They are all formed by the auxiliary verb **haben** *(to have)* or **sein** *(to be)* + the past participle. You must memorize which verbs require **sein** and which require **haben** as the auxiliary in the perfect tenses.

PERFECT TENSE—**haben** *(to have)* or **sein** *(to be)* in the present tense + past participle of the main verb.

> Wir **sind** ins Kino **gegangen**.
> *We **have gone** to the movies* or *We **went** to the movies.*

> Wir **haben** den Film **gesehen**.
> *We **have seen** the film* or *We **saw** the film.*

Although this tense is structurally similar to the English present perfect, often it is best translated into English by a simple past.

> Ich **habe gegessen**.
> I   have   eaten
> *I ate.*
> simple past

Sometimes an adverb of past time will help you select how to translate a German verb in the perfect tense.

> **Gestern habe** ich zuviel **gegessen**.
> *Yesterday I ate too much.*
> adverb of past time + simple past

> [Awkward: "Yesterday I *have eaten* too much."]

Ich **habe schon** zuviel **gegessen**.
I have already eaten too much.
adverb of past time + present perfect

[Awkward: "I already *ate* too much."]

You will need to study your German textbook for more detailed explanations of the uses of the German perfect.

PAST PERFECT OR PLUPERFECT—**haben** *(to have)* or **sein** *(to be)* in the simple past tense + past participle of the main verb.

Wir **waren** schon ins Kino **gegangen**.
simple past of **sein** *(to be)*
*We **had** already **gone** to the movies.*

Wir **hatten** den Film schon **gesehen**.
simple past of **haben** *(to have)*
*We **had** already **seen** the film.*

This tense resembles the English past perfect both in structure and in use. It expresses an action or condition that has ended before some other past action or condition. Notice how we can express the sequence of events by using different tenses:

Verb tense:	Past perfect	Perfect or simple past	Present
	-2	-1	0
Time action takes place:	before -1	before 0	now

*They **had** already **left** when I **arrived**.*
Sie **waren** schon **abgefahren**, als ich **ankam**.
pluperfect -2   simple past -1

*After we **had eaten**, we took a walk.*
Nachdem wir **gegessen hatten**, **machten** wir einen Spaziergang.
pluperfect -2   simple past -1

FUTURE PERFECT—**haben** *(to have)* or **sein** *(to be)* in the future tense + past participle of the main verb.

Wir **werden** den Film **gesehen haben**.

future tense **haben**

*We **will have seen** the film.*

This tense is used like the English future perfect. It expresses an action which will be completed in the future before some other specific action or event occurs in the future.

Verb tense:	Present	Future perfect	Future
	0	1	2
Time action takes place:	now	after 0 and before 2	after 0 and 1

Let us look at an example.

*They **will have left** before I arrive.*
Sie **werden abgefahren sein**, bevor ich ankomme.

future perfect (1)   event in future (2)

Both action (1) and event (2) will occur at some future time, but action (1) will be completed before event (2) takes place. Therefore, action (1) is in the future perfect tense.

You will have to learn to recognize these tenses because they indicate the sequence in which events take place.

▼▼▼▼▼▼▼▼▼▼▼▼▼▼▼▼▼REVIEW▼▼▼▼▼▼▼▼▼▼▼▼▼▼▼▼▼

Underline the complete verbs in each sentence.
- Circle the number corresponding to the tense that indicates the sequence in time when the action takes place: 0 → present
                                                                                                -1 → simple past or present perfect
                                                                                                - 2 → past perfect

1. After they had said goodbye, they climbed into the car.

    0   -1   -2   0   -1   -2

2. She wants to know who called last night.

    0   -1   -2   0   -1   -2

22. WHAT IS THE FUTURE TENSE?

The **future tense** is used to describe an action which will take place in the future.

IN ENGLISH
The future tense is formed with the auxiliary verb *will* or *shall* + the main verb. Note that *shall* is used in formal English (and British English); *will* occurs in everyday language.

> Mary and Paul *will do* their homework tomorrow.
> I *shall go* out tonight.

In conversation, *shall* and *will* are often shortened to *'ll*: *they'll do it tomorrow, I'll go out tonight.*

Often the present tense is used in English to express a future action. When this occurs, an adverb helps express the sense of future time.

> We fly to Frankfurt *next week.*
> The semester ends *soon.*

IN GERMAN
The future tense is formed by the auxiliary verb **werden** (literally *to become*) + the infinitive of the main verb. The conjugated verb **werden** agrees with the subject and the infinitive remains unchanged.

> Mary und Paul **werden** ihre Hausaufgabe **schreiben**.
> | |
>   3rd per. pl.   infinitive
> *Mary and Paul **will write** their homework.*

> Ich **werde** heute abend **ausgehen**.
> | |
>   1st per. sing.   infinitive
> *I **shall go** out tonight.*

Note the word order in the above German sentences—the infinitive stands at the end of the sentence.

The future tense is used in two ways in German:

1. to express an action that will take place in the future.

> Wir **werden vorbeikommen**.
> |
>   werden + infinitive **vorbeikommen** (*to come*)
> *We **will come** by.*

Ich **werde anrufen**.

werden + infinitive **anrufen** *(to call)*
I will call.

Quite often, however, instead of using the future tense, German will use the present tense with an adverb of future time. We do this in English too, but less frequently.

Mary und Paul **schreiben morgen** ihre Prüfung.

present + adverb of future time

*Mary and Paul **are writing** their test **tomorrow**.*

Ich **gehe gleich** aus.

present + adverb of future time

*I **am going** out **soon**.*

2. to express an action that might take place in the future, sometimes called the **future of probability**. In such usage, the future tense has no future meaning, it refers simply to a probability in the present time.

The future of probability is usually expressed with the future tense and the adverbs **wohl** *(probably)*, **sicher** *(certainly)*, **wahrscheinlich** *(probably)*, and **vielleicht** *(perhaps)* to express probability. In such sentences the German future tense is best translated with the English present.

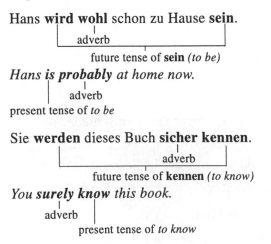

Hans **wird wohl** schon zu Hause **sein**.

adverb

future tense of **sein** *(to be)*

*Hans **is probably** at home now.*

adverb

present tense of *to be*

Sie **werden** dieses Buch **sicher kennen**.

adverb

future tense of **kennen** *(to know)*

*You **surely know** this book.*

adverb

present tense of *to know*

▼▼▼▼▼▼▼▼▼▼▼▼▼▼▼▼▼REVIEW▼▼▼▼▼▼▼▼▼▼▼▼▼▼▼▼▼

To help you think about the different ways in which German expresses the future and uses the future construction, look at these sentences in English.
- Underline the verbs in future tense.
- Circle the verbs in the present tense which are used with an adverb of future time.
- Box in the sentences which will use the future of probability in German.

1. Next week we are going on vacation.

2. Erica is probably downtown.

3. I shall return.

4. Only time will tell.

5. He'll be here in a minute.

6. The tickets probably cost a lot.

23. WHAT IS MEANT BY MOOD?

The word **mood** is a variation of the word *mode,* meaning manner or way. The mood is expressed by a form of the verb that indicates the attitude of the speaker toward what he or she is saying. As a beginning student of German, you need to know the names of the moods so that you will understand what your German textbook is referring to when it uses these terms. Verb forms are divided into moods, which, in turn, are then subdivided into one or more tenses. You will learn when to use the various moods as you learn verbs and their tenses.

IN ENGLISH

Verbs can be in one of three moods:

INDICATIVE MOOD—The indicative mood is used to indicate an action of the verb that really happens or is likely to happen. This is the most common mood, and most of the verb forms that you use in everyday conversation belong to the indicative mood.

> Robert *studies* German.
> Mary *is* here.

The indicative mood occurs in the present tense (see p. 63), the past tense (see p. 65), and the future tense (see p. 83).

IMPERATIVE MOOD—The imperative mood is used to express a command. The imperative mood does not have different tenses (see p. 88).

> Robert, *study* German now!
> Mary, *be* here on time!

SUBJUNCTIVE MOOD—The subjunctive mood is used to express an attitude or feeling about the action of the verb. Since it stresses feelings about what occurs in a sentence, it is "subjective." The subjunctive mood has different tense forms (see p. 90).

> I wish she *were* here.
> If only we *knew* where they are.
> The teacher recommended that they *do* the exercise.

IN GERMAN

These same three moods exist and have their own special forms. Although the indicative is the most common mood, as it is in English, the subjunctive is also very important.

▼▼▼▼▼▼▼▼▼▼▼▼▼▼▼▼▼REVIEW▼▼▼▼▼▼▼▼▼▼▼▼▼▼▼▼▼

Imagine how a speaker might say each sentence and indicate the mood of the verbs in *italics*: indicative (I), imperative (IM), or subjunctive (S).

1. Columbus *discovered* America.   I   IM   S

2. We wish you *were* here.   I   IM   S

3. *Come* into the house, children!   I   IM   S

4. We *have* bats in the attic.   I   IM   S

5. *Look* at that!   I   IM   S

24. WHAT IS THE IMPERATIVE?

The **imperative** is the mood of the verb used to give someone an order.

IN ENGLISH
There are two types of commands, depending on who is being told to do, or not to do, something.

"YOU COMMAND"—To give an order to one person or many persons, the dictionary form of the verb (see p. 55) is used.

> *Answer* the phone.
> *Clean* your room.
> *Talk* softly.

Notice that the pronoun "you" is not stated in these sentences, although it could be included for emphasis (i.e., *You,* clean your room right now!). The absence of the pronoun *you* in a sentence is a good indication that you are dealing with an imperative and not the present tense.

"WE COMMAND"—When an order is given to oneself as well as to others, the phrase "let's" + the dictionary form of the verb is used.

> *Let's leave.*
> *Let's go* to the movies.

IN GERMAN
As in English, there are two types of imperatives, depending on who is being told to do or not to do something.

"YOU COMMAND"—The *you*-command has three different forms, according to the three different personal pronouns for *you*: **du, ihr,** and **Sie** (see **What is a Personal Pronoun?**, p. 40). In all forms except the **du**-form, the verb is the same as the present tense indicative. In written German an exclamation mark is used after an imperative.

In the two familiar forms of the imperative (**du** and **ihr**), the subject pronoun is usually dropped, as in English:

- **du**-form

> **Höre!**[1]
> *Listen.*
>
> **Schreibe** mir bald!
> *Write me soon.*

---

[1] The final **-e** on **höre** and **schreibe** is optional in conversational German, though mandatory when the verb stem ends in **-t, -d,** or **-ig.**

- **ihr**-form

> **Kommt** mit!
> *Come along.*

> **Eßt** nicht so schnell, Kinder!
> *Don't eat so fast, children.*

In the formal form, the subject pronoun **Sie** is included; it is placed directly after the **Sie** form of the verb in the present tense.

- **Sie**-form

> **Sprechen Sie** lauter!
> *Speak more loudly.*

> **Kommen Sie** mit!
> *Come along.*

"WE COMMAND"—In the *we*-command, the subject pronoun **wir** is included; it is placed directly after the **wir**-form of the verb in the present tense.

- **wir**-form

> **Gehen wir** jetzt!
> *Let's go now.*

> **Sprechen wir** Deutsch!
> *Let's speak German.*

Your German textbook will explain in detail the rules for forming the imperative.

▼▼▼▼▼▼▼▼▼▼▼▼▼▼▼▼REVIEW▼▼▼▼▼▼▼▼▼▼▼▼▼▼▼▼▼

Indicate the imperative form you would use when translating these sentences into German: **du**, **ihr**, **Sie**, or **wir**.

1. Hurry up, Chris.	**du**	**ihr**	**Sie**	**wir**
2. Let's go to the movies.	**du**	**ihr**	**Sie**	**wir**
3. Close the door, children.	**du**	**ihr**	**Sie**	**wir**
4. Excuse me a minute, Dr. Benn.	**du**	**ihr**	**Sie**	**wir**
5. Please pick up your room, Ann.	**du**	**ihr**	**Sie**	**wir**

25. WHAT IS THE SUBJUNCTIVE?

The **subjunctive** is the mood of the verb which is used to express actions and conditions that are not actual fact. We often say that these actions are "unreal" or "contrary to fact," that is, that they are imaginary or hypothetical. Notice the difference between the indicative mood (used to express facts) and the subjunctive mood in the following examples:

INDICATIVE

■ states a fact

> Kathy *is* here.

■ states a real possibility, something that can be a fact

> If Kathy *is* here, you can meet her.
>> Implication: There is a real possibility that Kathy is here, and therefore that you can meet her.

SUBJUNCTIVE

■ expresses something that is unreal, **contrary to fact**

> If Kathy *were* here, you could meet her.
>> Implication: Kathy is not here, and you cannot meet her. Therefore this sentence is contrary to fact.

■ expresses a wish, i.e., a hypothetical condition

> I wish Kathy *were* here.
>> Implication: She is not here. Therefore this sentence expresses a hypothetical condition.

■ expresses necessity or demand

> We asked Kathy to *be* here so that we can meet her.
>> Implication: She is not here now and we are not certain that she will be here, but we urged her to come so that we could meet her.

IN ENGLISH

The subjunctive forms are difficult to identify because they resemble the forms of some tenses in the indicative. For this reason we do not always recognize verb forms as being subjunctive when we use them.

The subjunctive mood can be expressed in two different ways in the present, depending on the type of sentence in which it is used: by a verb form derived from the simple past (see p. 65), or by a verb form identical to the dictionary form (see p. 55).

SUBJUNCTIVE DERIVED FROM THE SIMPLE PAST—The contrast between the simple past indicative and the subjunctive is most evident in the verb *to be* in the lst and 3rd persons singular.

"To be"

Simple past		Present Subjunctive	
I	**was**	I	**were**
you	were	you	were
he, she, it	**was**	he, she it	**were**
we	were	we	were
you	were	you	were
they	were	they	were

With other verbs, you will have to rely on the meaning of the sentence to determine whether the verb is in the indicative or subjunctive mood because the forms of the simple past indicative and subjunctive are identical.

This subjunctive form occurs most commonly in two types of sentences:

- conditions contrary to fact—These sentences are made up of two clauses, the *if*-clause and the conclusion:

>   if-clause   conclusion
> If I *were* in Europe now, I would visit Vienna.

The verb of the *if*-clause is in the subjunctive; the verb of the conclusion clause, i.e., *would* + the dictionary form of the main verb, is in what is often called the **conditional**.

>   if-clause   conclusion
> If they *spoke* German, they *would go* with us.
>   subjunctive   conditional

- expressions of wishes

> I wish I *were* in Europe right now.
>   subjunctive

> If only we *spoke* German fluently!
>   subjunctive

Notice that the verb *wish* is used only in the first example. In the second example the wish is implied and the verb is in the subjunctive.

SUBJUNCTIVE IDENTICAL TO THE DICTIONARY FORM—This form is used with verbs for asking, urging, demanding, or requesting. Let us see how this subjunctive form compares with the present indicative.

> She *comes* to see me every week.
> |
>   fact
>   present indicative of the verb *to come*

> I asked that she *come* see me every week.
> | |
> demand   present subjunctive
>   infinitive of the verb *to come*

> He *is* here.
> |
>   fact
> present indicative of the verb *to be*

> It is necessary that he *be* here.
> |_____|_____|
>   demand   present subjunctive
>   infinitive of the verb *to be*

IN GERMAN

German subjunctive forms are much easier to identify than English ones because they are usually different from the German indicative forms. As in English, there are two different types of subjunctives, one derived from the simple past of the verb and one derived from the infinitive, but their usage is not the same as the usage of the two English subjunctive forms. In this section we will discuss only the first type, i.e., the one derived from the simple past, the so-called **general subjunctive** or **subjunctive II**, which has a present and a past tense. The other, less common, type of subjunctive is discussed in the section **What is Meant by Direct and Indirect Discourse?**, p. 97.

General Subjunctive (Subjunctive II)

Like the English subjunctive, German derives the general subjunctive form from the simple past form of the indicative.

PRESENT SUBJUNCTIVE—The present tense general subjunctive is formed by using the indicative past stem of the verb + subjunctive endings. The past stem of the verb is the stem to which you add the personal endings when you conjugate a verb in the simple past tense.

Infinitive		Past tense indicative (3rd per. sing.)		Past stem
sagen	*to say*	sagte	*said*	sagt-
schlafen	*to sleep*	schlief	*slept*	schlief-

Let us look at an example that shows the endings used to form the subjunctive in German:

Infinitive		Past tense		Past stem
gehen	*to go*	ging	*went*	ging-

Present general subjunctive

ich	ginge
du	gingest
er, sie, es	ginge
wir	gingen
ihr	ginget
sie, Sie	gingen

PAST SUBJUNCTIVE—The past subjunctive is a compound tense and resembles the German past perfect, except that the auxiliary verb (**haben** or **sein**) is in the subjunctive rather than in the indicative.[1]

ich	hätte	gesagt
du	hättest	gesagt
er, sie, es	hätte	gesagt
wir	hätten	gesagt
ihr	hättet	gesagt
sie, Sie	hätten	gesagt
ich	wäre	gekommen
du	wärest	gekommen
er, /sie, es	wäre	gekommen
wir	wären	gekommen
ihr	wäret	gekommen
sie, Sie	wären	gekommen

As a student of German, you will need to learn many details about general subjunctive usage and the verb forms that are exceptions. Your textbook will give you a detailed explanation of all the subjunctive forms and the special rules you need to follow when using them.

The general subjunctive is commonly used in three kinds of sentences:

- expressions contrary to fact—Unlike English, where the subjunctive is used only in the *if*-clause, in German the subjunctive is also used in the conclusion where the English verb is in the *would*-construction, i.e., the conditional.

[1]Note that while the indicative mood in German has three tenses to express actions in the past (past, perfect, and past perfect), the subjunctive mood has only one past form.

        if-clause   conclusion

*If she **were** here, I **would be** happy.*

        subjunctive   conditional

Wenn sie hier **wäre**, dann **wäre** ich glücklich.

        subjunctive   subjunctive

        if-clause   conclusion

*If we **had been** more intelligent, we **would have learned** faster.*

        subjunctive   conditional

Wenn wir intelligenter **gewesen wären**,

        subjunctive

        dann **hätten** wir schneller **gelernt**.

        subjunctive

- expressions of wishes—Unlike English, where the subjunctive is used only in the conclusion of the wish-statement, in German the verb *wish* is also in the subjunctive.

  *I **wish** she **were** here!*

  indicative subjunctive

  Ich **wünschte**, sie **wäre** doch hier!

    subjunctive   subjunctive

  *I **wish** I **were** in Europe now!*

  indicative subjunctive

  Ich **wünschte**, ich **wäre** jetzt in Europa!

    subjunctive   subjunctive

- polite requests

  ***Could** you **do** me a favor?*
  Könntest du mir einen Gefallen **tun**?

  subjunctive   infinitive

  ***Would** you please **open** the door?.*
  Würden Sie bitte die Tür **aufmachen**?

  subjunctive   infinitive

The würde-**Construction**

German also has a two-word construction, called the **würde**-construction, which often replaces the one-word general subjunctive forms in spoken German. The **würde**-construction is formed by the present general subjunctive form of **werden** (literally *to become*) + the infinitive.

ich	würde	gehen
du	würdest	gehen
er, sie, es	würde	gehen
wir	würden	gehen
ihr	würdet	gehen
sie, Sie	würden	gehen

In structure, German sentences using the **würde**-construction resemble sentences in English formed using *would* + the dictionary form of the main verb, i. e., the conditional (see p. 91).

Ich **würde gehen**, wenn ich Zeit hätte.

subjunctive of **werden**   subjunctive of **haben** *(to have)*
+ infinitive **gehen** *(to go)*
*I **would go** if I had time.*

Sie **würden** dich **einladen**, wenn sie könnten.

subjunctive of **werden**   subjunctive of **können** *(to be able to)*
+ infinitive **einladen** *(to invite)*
*They **would invite** you if they could.*

Note that in both English and German this subjunctive structure resembles the future indicative construction (see **What is the Future Tense?**, p. 83).

Ich **werde gehen**.	Ich **würde gehen**.
present of **werden**	subjunctive of **werden**
*I **will go**.*	*I **would go**.*

Your textbook will explain when you should use this construction and when you must use the one-word general subjunctive forms.

As you learn more German, you will discover various other situations in which the subjunctive is used. Although its use does not always resemble that of the English subjunctive, being aware of the subjunctive in English can often help you use it correctly in German.

▼▼▼▼▼▼▼▼▼▼▼▼▼▼▼▼▼▼REVIEW▼▼▼▼▼▼▼▼▼▼▼▼▼▼▼▼▼▼

I. Indicate whether each of the following statements is a statement of fact
    (F) or contrary to fact (CTF).

1. West Germany is approximately the size of Oregon.   F   CTF

2. I wish I were finished already.   F   CTF

3. If I had wings, I would fly away.   F   CTF

4. Since things are going smoothly, we will be done soon.   F   CTF

5. If they had come earlier, we could have gone for a walk.   F   CTF

II. Underline the verbs in the following sentences.
▪ Indicate the tense you would use to express these sentences in German:
  present (P) or past (PA).

1. If only Reinhard were back!   P   PA

2. Students would do their homework if they had time.   P   PA

3. If we had planned ahead,

   we would have packed warmer clothes.   P   PA

4. I would like a glass of mineral water.   P   PA

5. If it were colder, I would wear gloves.   P.   PA

6. If she had called, I would have come.   P   PA

7. If only the rain had stopped already!   P   PA

26. WHAT IS MEANT BY DIRECT AND INDIRECT DISCOURSE?

Direct discourse is the transmission of another person's statement or message by direct quotation. Direct discourse is usually set in quotation marks.

> Mary said, "I am going to Berlin."
> John asked, "What will you do in Berlin?"

The words that appear in quotation marks are what you would hear if you eavesdropped on a conversation.

Indirect discourse is the transmission of another person's statement or message without quoting their words directly. Indirect discourse reproduces the substance of the message but does not use quotation marks. Furthermore, it changes the speaker's first-person pronoun (*"I* am going..."*) to agree logically with the perspective of the person speaking (*"She* was going...").

> Mary said *she was going to Berlin.*
> John asked *what she would do in Berlin.*

If you were reporting a conversation you overheard, you would automatically change the pronouns in this manner. This is what happens in indirect discourse.

IN ENGLISH
Indirect discourse is often indicated by a shift in tense.

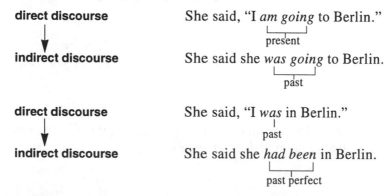

direct discourse   She said, "I *am going* to Berlin."
                                            present

indirect discourse   She said she *was going* to Berlin.
                                            past

direct discourse   She said, "I *was* in Berlin."
                                            past

indirect discourse   She said she *had been* in Berlin.
                                            past perfect

IN GERMAN
Indirect discourse is indicated by a shift in mood from the indicative to the subjunctive. There is a **special subjunctive** called the **indirect discourse subjunctive** or **subjunctive I** which is used primarily for

indirect discourse in writing. In conversation the general subjunctive or subjunctive II is often used for indirect discourse (see p. 92). The special subjunctive has a present and past tense.

Let us look at how the special subjunctive is formed and how German uses both the special subjunctive (in writing) and the general subjunctive (in conversation) to express indirect discourse in the present and past tenses.

PRESENT—The present tense of the special subjunctive is formed by the infinitive stem + the subjunctive endings.

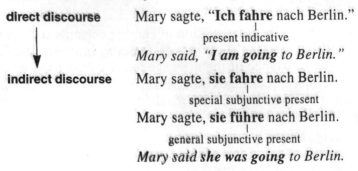

direct discourse   Mary sagte, "**Ich fahre** nach Berlin."

present indicative

Mary said, "I am going to Berlin."

indirect discourse   Mary sagte, **sie fahre** nach Berlin.

special subjunctive present

Mary sagte, **sie führe** nach Berlin.

general subjunctive present

Mary said she was going to Berlin.

PAST—The past tense is formed by the special subjunctive form of the helping verb (**haben** or **sein**) + the past participle of the main verb.

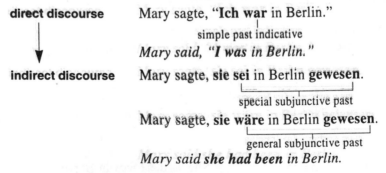

direct discourse   Mary sagte, "**Ich war** in Berlin."

simple past indicative

Mary said, "I was in Berlin."

indirect discourse   Mary sagte, **sie sei** in Berlin **gewesen**.

special subjunctive past

Mary sagte, **sie wäre** in Berlin **gewesen**.

general subjunctive past

Mary said she had been in Berlin.

Your German textbook will explain in greater detail the formation and use of the special indirect discourse subjunctive.

▼▼▼▼▼▼▼▼▼▼▼▼▼▼▼▼REVIEW▼▼▼▼▼▼▼▼▼▼▼▼▼▼▼▼

Underline the verbs in the quotations below.
- Indicate whether the verb describes an action in the present (P) or in the past (PA).
- Box in any pronouns or possessive adjectives within the quotation that will change when these sentences are in indirect discourse.
- Rewrite these direct discourse sentences as indirect discourse.

1. She asked, "How is the weather?"   P   PA

   She asked _____

2. They shouted, "We found the trail."   P   PA

   They shouted that _____

3. He announced, "I just got my driver's license."   P   PA

   He announced that _____

4. Libby said, "I'm coming."   P   PA

   Libby said that _____

5. Tony called out, "I'm done."   P   PA

   Tony called out that _____

27. WHAT IS A POSSESSIVE PRONOUN?

A **possessive pronoun** is a word that both replaces a noun and indicates the possessor of that noun. The word *possessive* comes from possess, to own.

IN ENGLISH

Here is a list of the possessive pronouns.

Singular possessor

1st person		mine
2nd person		yours
3rd person	{ masculine	his
	feminine	hers
	neuter	its

Plural possessor

1st person	ours
2nd person	yours
3rd person	theirs

Possessive pronouns only refer to the possessor; they never change their form, regardless of the thing possessed.

John's car is blue. *His* is blue.
Mary's car is blue. *Hers* is blue.

> Although the object possessed is the same *(car)*, the possessive pronoun is different because the possessor is different *(John* is masculine singular; *Mary* is feminine singular).

Is that your house? Yes, it is *mine.*
Are those your keys? Yes, they are *mine.*

> The same possessive pronoun *(mine)* is used, although the objects possessed are different in number *(house* is singular; *keys* is plural).

IN GERMAN

As in English, the possessive pronouns refer to the possessor, but they also must agree in case, gender, and number with the object possessed; i.e., noun they replace. The case endings are added on to the various stems of the possessive pronouns.

Singular possessor

1st person		mein-
2nd person	informal	dein-
	formal	Ihr-
3rd person	masculine	sein-
	feminine	ihr-
	neuter	sein-

Plural possessor

1st person		unser-
2nd person	informal	euer-
	formal	Ihr-
3rd person		ihr-

The forms of the possessive pronouns are essentially the same as those of the possessive adjectives (see **What is a Possessive Adjective?**, p. 133), but the endings are slightly different. Note that a possessive pronoun stands by itself in a sentence while the possessive adjective precedes the noun it modifies.

Possessive adjective	**Possessive pronoun**
Das ist **mein** Buch.	Das ist **meins**.
adjective noun	pronoun
*That is **my** book.*	*That is **mine**.*
Hier ist **unser** Bleistift.	Hier ist **unserer**.
adjective noun	pronoun
*Here is **our** pencil.*	*Here is **ours**.*

▼▼▼▼▼▼▼▼▼▼▼▼▼▼▼▼REVIEW▼▼▼▼▼▼▼▼▼▼▼▼▼▼▼▼▼

Circle the possessive pronouns in the following sentences.

1. I have my book; do you have yours?

2. Did your parents come? Ours stayed home.

3. Whose report was the best? Hers was.

4. Did somebody forget this jacket? Yes, it's his.

5. Let me see those keys: I bet they're mine.

28. WHAT IS A REFLEXIVE PRONOUN?

A **reflexive pronoun** is a pronoun which refers back to the subject of the sentence: it *reflects* the meaning back to the subject. Both the subject and the pronoun refer to the same person(s), thing(s), or idea(s).

IN ENGLISH
Reflexive pronouns end with *-self* in the singular and *-selves* in the plural:

	Subject pronoun	Reflexive pronoun
singular	I	my*self*
	you	your*self*
	he	him*self*
	she	her*self*
	it	it*self*
plural	we	our*selves*
	you	your*selves*
	they	them*selves*

Reflexive pronouns agree in person and number with their antecedents and *he*, *she*, and *it* also agree in gender. This is because the reflexive pronoun and the subject refer to the same person, thing, or idea.

> I washed *myself.*
> Mark and Gretchen helped *themselves* to dessert.

Although the subject pronoun *you* is the same for the singular and plural, there is a difference in the reflexive pronouns used to refer to these subjects: *yourself* (singular) is used when speaking to one person and *yourselves* (plural) when speaking to more than one person.

> Molly, did you make *yourself* a sandwich?
> Children, make sure you dry *yourselves* properly.

A reflexive pronoun can have various functions in a sentence, such as:

- a reflexive pronoun can be a direct object

> I cut *myself* with the knife.
> | |
> subject   direct object

> > Who cut herself with the knife? I did.
> > *I* is the subject of the sentence.

Whom did I cut with the knife? Myself.
Myself is the direct object of the verb *cut.*

I can't help *myself.*
| |
subject   direct object

Who can't help himself? I can't.
I is the subject of the sentence.
Whom can I not help? Myself.
Myself is the direct object of the verb *help.*

- a reflexive pronoun can be an indirect object

You should write *yourself* a note.
| |
subject   indirect object

Who should write herself a note? You should.
You is the subject of the sentence.
To whom should you write a note? To yourself.
Yourself is the indirect object of the verb *write.*
What should you write yourself? A note.
Note is the direct object of the verb *write.*

- a reflexive pronoun can be an object of a preposition

He thinks only of *himself.*
| |
subject   object of preposition

Who thinks only of himself? He does.
He is the subject of the sentence.
Of whom does he think? Of himself.
Himself is the object of the preposition *of.*

They talk about *themselves* too much.
| |
subject   object of preposition

Who spoke about themselves? They did.
They is the subject of the sentence.
About whom did they speak? About themselves.
Themselves is the object of the preposition *about.*

IN GERMAN

As in English there are reflexive pronouns for each of the different
personal pronouns (1st, 2nd, and 3rd persons, singular and plural). The
German reflexive pronouns, however, have both an accusative form
(for direct objects and for prepositions that require the accusative) and
a dative form (for indirect objects and for prepositions that require the

dative). Depending on the verb or the preposition, you will choose either the accusative or the dative reflexive pronoun.

SUBJECT PRONOUN nominative	REFLEXIVE PRONOUN accusative	dative	
ich	mich	mir	*myself*
du	dich	dir	*yourself*
er, sie, es	sich	sich	*himself herself itself*
wir	uns	uns	*ourselves*
ihr	euch	euch	*yourselves*
sie	sich	sich	*themselves*
Sie	sich	sich	*yourself (-selves)*

A reflexive pronoun in German can function as different types of objects:

- the direct or indirect object of the verb

  *I cut **myself** with the knife.*
  direct object of *cut*
      You cut whom? Yourself → direct object
  Ich habe **mich** mit dem Messer geschnitten.
  subject   accusative object of **geschnitten** *(to cut)*

  *You should write **yourself** a note.*
  indirect object of *write*
      You should write to whom? To yourself → indirect object
  Du solltest **dir** einen Zettel schreiben.
  subject dative object accusative object
              of **schreiben** *(to write)*

- the object of a preposition

  *He thinks only of **himself**.*
  object of preposition *of*
      Remember: *to think of* → **denken an** + accusative
  Er denkt nur an **sich**.
  subject   accusative object of **denken an**

*You talk about **yourself** too much.*

       object of preposition *about*

     Remember: *to talk about* → **reden von** + dative

Du redest zuviel von **dir**.

subject   dative object of **von**

Careful

When German reflexive pronouns are used as objects of verbs and as objects of prepositions, you will need to pay attention to the case required. Remember that the case of the reflexive pronoun depends on its function in the German sentence, not the English sentence. Pay special attention to verbs that take a direct object in English, but require a dative case in German.

*I can't help **myself**.*

  direct object of *help*

     Remember: *to help* → **helfen** + dative

Ich kann **mir** nicht helfen.

subject dative object of **helfen**

▼▼▼▼▼▼▼▼▼▼▼▼▼▼▼▼▼▼▼REVIEW▼▼▼▼▼▼▼▼▼▼▼▼▼▼▼▼▼▼▼

Fill in the proper reflexive pronoun.

1. Ruby, you should feel free to make _____ at home.

2. We fixed the car _____.

3. He picked everything up by _____.

4. She wanted some time to _____.

5. I wish I'd thought of that _____.

6. Maura and Steve, you should get _____ ready.

29. WHAT IS A REFLEXIVE VERB?

A **reflexive verb** is a verb linked to a special pronoun called a reflexive pronoun (see **What is a Reflexive Pronoun?**, p. 102).

IN ENGLISH

Many verbs can take on a reflexive meaning by adding a reflexive pronoun.

> Marlene *cuts* the paper.
> regular verb

> Peter *cuts himself* when he shaves.
> verb + reflexive pronoun

There are very few verbs, however, that require a reflexive pronoun to complete their meaning. Verbs which can have a reflexive pronoun as their object can also have other nouns or pronouns as their object.

> I hurt *myself*.
> reflexive pronoun as direct object

> I don't like to hurt *people*.
> noun as direct object

> Please, calm *yourself*.
> reflexive pronoun as direct object

> The soft music calmed his *nerves*.
> noun as direct object

IN GERMAN

There are some verbs that must have reflexive pronouns to complete their meaning. These verbs are called **reflexive verbs**. The English equivalents of these verbs do not have reflexive pronouns.

sich erhohlen	*to recover*
sich befinden	*to be located*
sich verlieben	*to fall in love*

As you can see, the infinitive of these verbs is always given with the third person reflexive pronoun, **sich**. When you conjugate a reflexive verb, you will also have to select the correct reflexive pronoun since it changes as the subject changes. Notice that the verb **sich erhohlen** (*to* *recover)*, conjugated below in the present tense, takes the accusative form of the reflexive pronoun.

Subject pronoun	Verb	Reflexive pronoun
ich	erhole	mich
du	erholst	dich
er	erholt	sich
sie	erholt	sich
es	erholt	sich
wir	erholen	uns
ihr	erholt	euch
sie	erholen	sich
Sie	erholen	sich

Reflexive verbs can be conjugated in all tenses. The subject pronoun and reflexive pronoun remain the same regardless of the verb tense; only the verb form changes: **du erhlolst dich** (present), **du wirst dich erholen** (future), **du hast dich erholt** (perfect).

Careful

As you learn new vocabulary, you will need to memorize which German verbs are reflexive, that is, which ones require the reflexive pronoun as part of the whole verb. A number of verbs can be used with or without reflexive pronouns, and sometimes verbs have a different meaning when they are reflexive. Your German textbook will introduce you to these verbs.

▼▼▼▼▼▼▼▼▼▼▼▼▼▼▼▼▼REVIEW▼▼▼▼▼▼▼▼▼▼▼▼▼▼▼▼▼

Using the sample conjugation above, fill in the accusative reflexive pronouns of the reflexive verb **sich freuen über** *(to be happy about something).*

ich freue   _____

du freust   _____

er, sie, es freut   _____

wir freuen   _____

ihr freut   _____

sie, Sie freuen   _____

30. WHAT IS AN INTERROGATIVE PRONOUN?

An **interrogative pronoun** is a word that replaces a noun and introduces a question. Interrogative comes from *interrogate*, meaning to question.

IN ENGLISH

Different interrogative pronouns are used depending on whether you are referring to a "person" (this category includes human beings and live animals) or a "thing" (this category includes objects and ideas). In addition, the interrogative pronoun referring to persons changes according to its function in the sentence.

"Person"

Who is the nominative form and stands for the subject of the sentence.

Who lives here?
subject

Who wrote that book?
subject

Whom is the objective form and is used as the object of a verb or, in standard written English, as the object of a preposition.

Whom do you know here?
direct object

From *whom* did you get the book?
preposition
        object of preposition

Whose is the possessive form and is used in questions about possession or ownership.

I found a pencil. *Whose* is it?
I have Mary's paper. *Whose* do you have?

Careful

In spoken or colloquial English we often use the nominative case *who* instead of the objective case *whom*.

Who do you know here? [*Whom* do you know here?]

Who did you get the book from? [From *whom* did you get the book?]

Since the interrogative pronoun *who* can function as both a subject and an object, it is important that you establish its function so that you will know which case to use in German.

"Thing"
What refers only to things, and the same form is used for the subject, the direct object, the indirect object, and the object of a preposition.[1]

What happened?
|
subject

What do you want?
|
direct object

What did you cook with?
|
object of preposition *with* [*With what* did you cook?]

IN GERMAN
As in English, different interrogative pronouns are used when referring to persons and when referring to things. In addition, the form of an interrogative pronoun depends on its case. (Number and gender do not affect the interrogative pronoun.) Let us look at the interrogative pronouns referring to persons first because they are more complicated.

"Person"
When referring to a person, there is a different interrogative pronoun for each case.

nominative	wer
accusative	wen
dative	wem
possessive	wessen

To select the proper form of the interrogative pronoun, you will have to determine its function in the German sentence by asking the following five questions.

1. Is it the subject of the question?
2. Is it the object of the verb? Does that verb take the accusative or the dative?
3. Is it the indirect object of the verb?

[1]Do not confuse with "*What* book is on the table?" where *what* is an interrogative adjective. See p.136.

4. Is it the object of the preposition? Does that preposition take the accusative or the dative?
5. Is it the possessive pronoun *whose*?

Here are examples of the interrogative pronoun in each of the five functions listed above.

1. Subject *(who)* → **nominative** → Wer?

Be sure to establish that the function of *who* is as the subject of the sentence and not as an object (see p. 108).

> *Who is in the room? The teacher is in the room.*
> > FUNCTION: subject of *is*
> > CASE: nominative

Wer ist in dem Zimmer? Die Lehrerin ist in dem Zimmer.

> *Who is coming this evening? Hans and Inge are coming.*
> > FUNCTION: subject of *is coming*
> > CASE: nominative

Wer kommt heute abend? Hans und Inge kommen.

As you can see, **wer** can refer to both singular and plural subjects. Number and gender do not affect the interrogative pronouns in German.

2. Object *(whom)* → **accusative** → Wen? *or* dative → Wem?

When *who* is functioning as an object, rather than as a subject, you can replace it with the correct form *whom* (see p. 108). You will then need to determine whether the German sentence requires the accusative or dative case.

> *Who do you see?* → *Whom do you see?*
> > FUNCTION: direct object of *see*
> > > *You* is the subject of *see*.
> > CASE: German verb **sehen** *(to see)* requires an accusative object.

Wen sehen Sie?
|
accusative

> *Who are they helping?* → *Whom are they helping?*
> > FUNCTION: direct object of *are helping*
> > > *They* is the subject of *are helping*.
> > CASE: German verb **helfen** *(to help)* requires a dative object.

Wem helfen sie?
|
dative

3. Indirect object *(whom)* → dative → Wem?

Be sure to distinguish *who* functioning as an indirect object from *who* functioning as a subject. To help you establish the function, restructure the English sentence so that the dangling preposition *to* precedes the interrogative pronoun (see p. 108).

> *Who is she sending a letter to? → To whom is she sending a letter?*
> FUNCTION: indirect object of *is sending*
> > *She* is the subject of *is sending.*
> > *A letter* is the direct object.
> CASE: dative
> **Wem** schickt sie einen Brief?

> *Who did you tell the story to? → To whom did you tell the story?*
> FUNCTION: indirect object of *did tell*
> > *You* is the subject of *did tell.*
> > *The story* is the direct object.
> CASE: dative
> **Wem** hast du die Geschichte erzählt?

The word **wem** means "to whom" or "for whom" an action is done; thus when it functions as an indirect object we do not need a preposition to complete its meaning as we do in English.

4. Object of a Preposition (preposition + *whom*) → preposition + accusative → wen? *or* preposition + dative → wem?

Be sure to distinguish *who* functioning as an object of a preposition from *who* functioning as a subject. To help you establish the function, restructure the English sentence so that the dangling preposition precedes the interrogative pronoun (see p. 108). Then, determine whether the German preposition requires the accusative or dative case.

> *Who are you doing that for? → For whom are you doing that?*
> FUNCTION: object of preposition
> > *You* is the subject of *are doing.*
> CASE: **Für** *(for)* requires an accusative object.
> **Für wen** machst du das?

> *Who are we going with? → With whom are we going?*
> FUNCTION: object of preposition
> > *We* is the subject of *are going.*
> CASE: **Mit** *(with)* requires a dative object.
> **Mit wem** gehen wir?

5. Possessive *(whose)* → genitive → Wessen?

This form should present no problems since the English form *whose* can be identified easily and there is only one form in German.

> ***Whose** pencil is that?*
> **Wessen** Bleistift ist das?
>
> ***Whose** house did you buy?*
> **Wessen** Haus habt ihr gekauft?

"Thing"

Was *(what)* is the only interrogative pronoun for asking about things. The same form is used for the nominative, dative, and accusative cases, and no distinction is made between the singular and the plural.

> ***What** is in this package?*
> subject
> **Was** ist in diesem Paket?
> nominative
>
> ***What** are you doing?*
> direct object
> **Was** machst du?
> accusative

▼▼▼▼▼▼▼▼▼▼▼▼▼▼▼▼REVIEW▼▼▼▼▼▼▼▼▼▼▼▼▼▼▼▼

Underline the interrogative pronouns in the following sentences, restructuring where appropriate.
- Indicate the type and function of the antecedent: Subject (S), Direct object (DO), Indirect object (IO), or Object of a preposition (OP).
- Write the appropriate German interrogative pronoun using the information given.

1. Who read the book?

   TYPE OF ANTECEDENT: Person   Thing

   FUNCTION: S   DO   IO   OP

   _____ hat das Buch gelesen.

2. What did she say?

   TYPE OF ANTECEDENT: Person   Thing

   FUNCTION: S   DO   IO   OP

   _____ hat sie gesagt?

3. Whose car is that?

   TYPE OF ANTECEDENT: Person   Thing

   FUNCTION: S   DO   IO   OP

   _____ Auto ist das?

4. Who are we waiting for?

   RESTRUCTURED: _____

   TYPE OF ANTECEDENT: Person   Thing

   FUNCTION: S   DO   IO   OP

   (*to wait for* = **warten auf** + accusative)

   Auf _____ warten wir?

31. WHAT IS A RELATIVE PRONOUN?

A **relative pronoun** is a word that serves two purposes:

1. As a pronoun it stands for a noun or another pronoun that has been mentioned previously. The noun or pronoun it refers to is called its **antecedent**.

> This is the boy *who* broke the window.
> |
> antecedent

2. As a relative pronoun it introduces a **relative clause**. A relative clause is a type of dependent (or subordinate) clause, that is, a group of words having a subject and a verb separate from the subject and verb of the main sentence (see **What is a Clause?**, p. 161). A dependent clause cannot stand alone as a complete sentence.

> main clause   dependent clause
> ┌──────────┐ ┌──────────────────┐
> This is the boy *who* broke the window.
> | |
>   subject verb

"Who broke the window" is not a complete sentence.

In this sentence *who* is a relative pronoun introducing the relative clause. The relative clause gives us additional information about the antecedent *boy*.

IN ENGLISH

The relative pronoun used depends on its function in the relative clause and, in some cases, on whether the antecedent is a "person" or a "thing" (see p. 49).

Let us look at the four functions of the English relative pronouns in a relative clause: 1. subject 2. direct object 3. indirect object and object of a preposition 4. possessive.

1. Subject of the Relative Clause

The relative pronoun subject of the relative clause is different depending on whether the antecedent refers to a person or a thing.

- antecedent refers to a person → *who*

> This is the student *who* answered all the time.
> |
>   antecedent

Who is the subject of *answered*.

- antecedent refers to a thing → *which*

    The plan, *which* was approved, is controversial.
    |
    antecedent
    Which is the subject of *was*.

- antecedent refers to a person or a thing → *that*

    This is the book *that* is so popular.
    |
    antecedent
    That is the subject of *is*.

2. Direct Object of the Relative Clause

The relative pronoun object in a relative clause is different depending on whether the antecedent refers to a person or a thing. Relative pronoun objects are often omitted in English, but we have indicated them in parentheses because they will have to be included in German.

- antecedent refers to a person → *whom*

    This is the student *(whom)* I saw yesterday.
    | |
    antecedent   direct object
    Whom is the direct object of *saw*.

- antecedent refers to a thing → *which*

    This is the book *(which)* I bought.
    | |
    antecedent direct object
    Which is the direct object of *bought*.

- antecedent refers to a person or a thing → *that*

    This is the book *(that)* I read.
    | | |
    antecedent   direct object
    That is the direct object of *read*.

3. Indirect Object or Object of a Preposition in the Relative Clause

The relative pronoun object in a relative clause is different depending on whether the antecedent refers to a person or a thing. Relative pronoun objects are often omitted in English, but we have indicated them in parentheses because they will have to be included in German. To parallel German structures, you will also need to restructure sentences to avoid the dangling prepositions common in spoken English (see p. 143).

- antecedent refers to a person → *whom*

   To avoid a dangling preposition and to establish the German structure, restructure the English sentence by inserting the preposition within the sentence and adding a relative pronoun. If you are not sure where to place the preposition and the relative pronoun, remember that they follow immediately after the antecedent.

   Let us look at some examples (the antecedent is in **bold**).

Spoken English	→	Restructured
Here is the **student**		Here is the **student**
I gave the present *to*.		*to whom* I gave the present.

   Whom is the indirect object of *gave*.

Spoken English	→	Restructured
Here is the **student**		Here is the **student**
I was speaking *about*.		*about whom* I was speaking.

   Whom is the object of the preposition *about*.

- antecedent refers to a thing → *which*

Spoken English	→	Restructured
Here is the **museum**		Here is the **museum**
they gave the painting *to*.		*to which* they gave the painting.

   Which is the indirect object of *gave*.

4. Possessive Modifier "Whose"

The possessive modifier *whose* is a relative pronoun that does not change its form regardless of its function or antecedent.

   Here are the people *whose* car was stolen.
   antecedent possessive modifying *car*

   Look at the house *whose* roof was fixed.
   antecedent possessive modifying *roof*

Careful

Remember that although the relative pronouns *who, whom, that*, and *which* are often omitted in English, they must always be stated in German. In English we can say either "Is that the house *that* Jack built?" or "Is that the house Jack built?" We can also say, "Is there anyone here *who(m)* you know?" or "Is there anyone here you know?" In German, only the first sentence in each of these pairs is possible.

IN GERMAN

Like nouns, German relative pronouns have four different case forms: nominative, accusative, dative, and genitive. The case used depends on the function of the pronoun in the relative clause. In German, it does not matter whether the antecedent is a person or a thing; the same set of relative pronouns refers to both. What is important is the gender and number of the antecedent; this will determine the gender and the number of the relative pronoun. The various forms of the relative pronoun are very similar to the forms of the definite article (**der, die, das**). Look at your German textbook to learn these forms.

To find the correct relative pronoun in German you must go through the following steps:

1. RELATIVE CLAUSE—Recognize the relative clause; restructure the English clause if there is a dangling preposition (see p. 143).
2. ANTECEDENT—Find the antecedent; i.e., to what word in the main clause does the relative clause refer? (Don't forget that the antecedent is always the noun that precedes the relative pronoun.)
3. NUMBER AND GENDER—Determine the number and gender of the antecedent.
   - Is it singular or plural?
   - If it is singular, is it masculine, feminine, or neuter?
   (There is only one plural for the three genders.)
4. FUNCTION—Determine the function and therefore the case of the relative pronoun within the relative clause:

		Case
• Is it the subject?	→	nominative
• Is it a direct object?	→	accusative
• Is it a dative object?	→	dative
• Is it an indirect object?	→	dative
• Is it the object of a preposition? What case does the preposition take	→	{ accusative dative genitive
• Is it a possessive modifier?	→	genitive

5. SELECTION—Select the proper form based on steps 1-4.

Let us apply these steps to select the relative pronoun in the following sentences.

*The man **who** visited us was nice.*

1. RELATIVE CLAUSE: *who* visited us
2. ANTECEDENT: man
3. NUMBER AND GENDER: **Der Mann** *(the man)* is masculine singular.
4. FUNCTION: subject → nominative
5. SELECTION: masculine singular nominative → **der**

Der Mann, **der** uns besuchte, war nett.

Is that the bike you bought?

1. RELATIVE CLAUSE: *(that)* you bought
   Remember that the relative pronoun must always be stated in German.
2. ANTECEDENT: the bike
3. NUMBER AND GENDER: **Das Rad** *(the bike)* is neuter singular.
4. FUNCTION: direct object → accusative
5. SELECTION: neuter singular accusative → **das**

Ist das das Rad, **das** du gekauft hast?

*Hans, **whose** alarm clock was broken, overslept.*

1. RELATIVE CLAUSE: *whose* alarm clock was broken
2. ANTECEDENT: Hans
3. NUMBER AND GENDER: Since Hans is the name of one man or boy, it is masculine singular.
4. FUNCTION: possessive modifier connecting *Hans* with *his alarm clock* → genitive
5. SELECTION: masculine singular genitive → **dessen**

Hans, **dessen** Wecker kaputt war, hat sich verschlafen.

Here are those books you were talking about.

Spoken English	→	Restructured
Here are those books you were talking *about.*		Here are those books *about which* you were talking.

1. RELATIVE CLAUSE: *about which* you were talking
2. ANTECEDENT: books
3. NUMBER AND GENDER: **Die Bücher** *(the books)* is neuter plural. (There is only one set of plural forms for all three genders.)
4. FUNCTION: object of preposition *about.* **Von** always takes a dative object.
5. SELECTION: neuter plural dative → **denen**

Hier sind die Bücher, von **denen** Sie geredet haben.

Relative pronouns are difficult to handle, and this handbook provides only a simple outline. Refer to your German textbook for further help.

Use of Relative Pronouns

Relative clauses are very common. We use them in everyday speech without giving much thought to why and how we construct them. Relative pronouns allow us to combine in a single sentence two thoughts that have a common element.

Let us look at a few examples.

sentence a: That is the player.
sentence b: He won the game.

1. COMMON ELEMENT—Identify the element the two sentences have in common.

    The player and *he*; both refer to the same person.
    The player (sentence A) is the antecedent.
    He (sentence B) will be replaced by a relative pronoun.

2. FUNCTION—Establish the function of the relative pronoun in the relative clause. It will have the same function as the word it replaces.

    The relative pronoun will be the subject of *won.* (*He* is the subject of *won.*)

3. PERSON OR THING—Choose the appropriate relative pronoun according to whether its antecedent is a person or a thing.

    Who is the relative pronoun referring to persons.

4. PLACEMENT—Place the relative pronoun after its antecedent.

    That is the player *who* won the game.
                 antecedent   relative clause

sentence a: The German teacher is new.
sentence b: I met her today.

    1. COMMON ELEMENT: *the German teacher* and *her*
    2. FUNCTION: direct object
    3. ANTECEDENT: *The German teacher* is a person. We can use *whom* as a relative pronoun.
    4. PLACEMENT: *whom* after *the German teacher*

The German teacher, *whom* I met today, is new.
        antecedent   relative clause

In spoken English, you would say: "The German teacher I met today is new." Notice that the relative pronoun *whom* would be left out, making it difficult to identify the two clauses.

sentence a: They had read the book.
sentence b: I was speaking about it.

1. COMMON ELEMENT: *book* and *it*
2. FUNCTION: object of the preposition *about*
3. ANTECEDENT: *The book* is not a person. We use the relative pronoun *which*.
4. PLACEMENT: *about which* after the *book*

They had read the book *about which* I was speaking.

         antecedent   relative clause

In spoken English, you would say: "They had read the book I was speaking about." Notice that the preposition *about* would come at the end of the sentence and that there would be no relative pronoun.

Relative Clauses With Indefinite Antecedents

In all of the above examples, we can identify one particular noun or pronoun in the main clause as the antecedent of the relative clause. When no such single antecedent is clearly apparent, the relative clause is said to have an **indefinite antecedent**.

IN ENGLISH

We avoid using relative pronouns which do not have a definite antecedent, especially in standard written English.

    main clause   relative clause

Anna invited us all, *which* we found nice.

Here we have a relative clause, but there is no clear antecedent. The relative clause refers to the entire idea expressed in the main clause.

IN GERMAN

It is perfectly acceptable to consider an entire clause as the antecedent of the relative clause. In such sentences the relative pronoun **was** is always used.

    main clause   relative clause

*Anna invited us all, **which** we found nice.*

    entire clause as antecedent   relative clause

Anna hat uns alle eingeladen, **was** wir nett gefunden haben.

There are other instances in German which require the use of **was** as a relative pronoun. Refer to your German textbook for examples.

Restrictive Clauses Versus Non-Restrictive Clauses

IN ENGLISH

The punctuation of relative clauses reflects a distinction between those clauses which are "restrictive" and those which are "non-restrictive."

A **restrictive clause** is a clause that restricts or limits the meaning of the antecedent; such a clause is essential to the meaning of the sentence and cannot be omitted without changing the sense of the whole sentence. It is not set off from the rest of the sentence by commas. A restrictive clause is introduced by *who, whom, which,* or *that.*

> Do you know the woman *who* won the prize?
>   antecedent   relative clause

> The relative clause is essential to identify the antecedent, *the woman.* Thus the clause is restrictive and is not set off by commas.

A **non-restrictive clause** is a clause that is not essential to the meaning of the sentence and which could be omitted without losing the sentence's basic meaning. It is set off from the rest of the sentence by commas. A non-restrictive clause is introduced by *who, whom, whose,* or *which.*

> My friend John, *whom* you met last week, is here.
>   antecedent   relative clause

> The relative clause is not essential to identify the antecedent; it merely gives additional information about *my friend John.* Thus the clause is non-restrictive and must be set off by commas.

Often in your own writing you can decide only from the context of the sentence whether a relative clause is restrictive or non-restrictive.

IN GERMAN

All German relative clauses, restrictive and non-restrictive, are separated by commas from the main clause of the sentence. As far as punctuation is concerned, there is no distinction between restrictive and nonrestrictive clauses.

▼▼▼▼▼▼▼▼▼▼▼▼▼▼▼▼▼REVIEW▼▼▼▼▼▼▼▼▼▼▼▼▼▼▼▼▼

I. Underline the relative pronoun in the following sentences.
- Circle its antecedent.
- Identify the function of the relative pronoun: subject (S) direct object (DO) indirect object (IO) object of a preposition (OP) possessive modifier (PM)

1. I received the letter that you sent me.   S   DO   IO   OP   PM

2. Those are the people who speak German.   S   DO   IO   OP   PM

3. The woman whom you met left today.   S   DO   IO   OP   PM

4. This is the book whose title I forgot.   S   DO   IO   OP   PM

5. Kit is the student about whom I spoke.   S   DO   IO   OP   PM

II. Circle the common elements in the following pairs of sentences.
- Fill in the information requested to find the relative pronoun.
- On the line below, write a new English sentence using a relative pronoun.

1. The dog is friendly. It lives next door.

   ANTECEDENT: _____ ELEMENT REPLACED:_____

   FUNCTION OF ELEMENT REPLACED:_____

   RELATIVE PRONOUN:_____

   _____

2. The Smiths left for Austria. You met them in Basel.

   ANTECEDENT: _____ ELEMENT REPLACED:_____

   FUNCTION OF ELEMENT REPLACED:_____

   RELATIVE PRONOUN:_____

   _____

3. The new student is German. You were asking about her.

   ANTECEDENT: _____ ELEMENT REPLACED:_____

   FUNCTION OF ELEMENT REPLACED:_____

   RELATIVE PRONOUN:_____

   _____

32. WHAT IS AN ADJECTIVE?

An **adjective** is a word that describes a noun or a pronoun.

IN ENGLISH

Adjectives are classified according to the way they describe a noun or pronoun.

DESCRIPTIVE ADJECTIVE—A descriptive adjective indicates a quality. It answers the question *what kind?* See p. 124.

> The house was *large*.
> The woman is *intelligent*.
> The *small* child plays in front of the *red* house.
> They are *nice*.

POSSESSIVE ADJECTIVE—A possessive adjective shows to whom or to what something belongs. It answers the question *whose?* See p. 133.

> *His* book is lost.
> *Our* parents are away.

INTERROGATIVE ADJECTIVE—An interrogative adjective forms a question about someone or something. It asks *which?* or *what?* See p. 136.

> *What* book is lost?
> *Which* newspaper do you want?

DEMONSTRATIVE ADJECTIVE—A demonstrative adjective points out someone or something. It answers the question *which one?*

> *This* teacher is excellent.
> *That* question is very appropriate.

In all these cases, it is said that the adjective *modifies* the noun or pronoun.

IN GERMAN

Adjectives are identified in the same way as in English. The form that an adjective takes, however, depends on the case, gender, and number of the noun it modifies. We will discuss descriptive, possessive, and interrogative adjectives in separate sections of this handbook. Your German textbook will introduce demonstrative adjectives, which you should learn as vocabulary items.

33. WHAT IS A DESCRIPTIVE ADJECTIVE?

A **descriptive adjective** is a word that indicates a quality of a noun or pronoun. As the name implies, it *describes* the noun or pronoun.

There are two types of descriptive adjectives: attributive adjectives and predicate adjectives.

An **attributive adjective** is an adjective which appears before the noun it modifies.

> the *small* child
> attributive adjective modifying the noun *child*

> the *red* house
> predicate adjective modifying the noun *house*

A **predicate adjective** is an adjective that accompanies a linking verb (see **What is a Predicate Noun?**, p. 32), often a form of the verb *to be*. A predicate adjective modifies the subject of the sentence.

> He is *small*.
> predicate adjective modifying the pronoun *he*

> The house is *red*.
> attributive adjective modifying the noun *house*

IN ENGLISH

A descriptive adjective has only one form, whether it is used as an attributive or predicate adjective.

> The *small* child sat in the sandbox.
> attributive adjective modifying *child*
>
> The child is *small*.
>   linking
>   verb
> subject   predicate adjective

> The *red* house is for sale.
> attributive adjective modifying *house*
>
> The house is *red*.
>   linking
>   verb
> subject   predicate adjective

The *tired* mother put her feet up.
attributive adjective modifying *mother*

I am getting *tired*.

    linking
    verb
subject   predicate adjective

IN GERMAN

The form of a descriptive adjective depends on whether it is used as an attributive adjective or as a predicate adjective. Attributive adjectives take special adjective endings; predicate adjectives do not.

ATTRIBUTIVE ADJECTIVES—To find the proper ending for an attributive adjective in German, you must ask yourself the following questions:

1. GENDER—What is the gender of the noun: masculine, feminine, or neuter?
2. NUMBER—Is the noun singular or plural in number?
3. CASE—What is the case of the noun: nominative, accusative, dative, or genitive?
4. ARTICLE—Is the noun preceded by a definite article, an indefinite article, or no article at all?

A German attributive adjective takes various sets of endings depending on how the case, gender, and number of the noun it modifies are indicated by the preceding article. When the article does not fully indicate the case, gender, and number, or when there is no article, an attributive adjective will have explicit, i.e., **"strong" endings**. These strong endings correspond to the forms of the definite article in the four cases (see p. 18). When the article itself clearly indicates case, gender, and number, an attributive adjective will take **"weak" endings**, i.e., less explicit ones. There are only two weak endings, **-e** and **-en**. By following the four steps above, you will be able to choose the appropriate ending for a given adjective. Your German textbook will show the various types of endings for you to memorize.

*The child plays in front of a **red** door.*

    ADJECTIVE: **rot** *(red)*
    GENDER: **Die Tür** *(the door)* is feminine.
    NUMBER: singular
    CASE: **vor** showing location takes dative
    ARTICLE: indefinite **eine** (dative form → **einer**)

Ein Kind spielt vor **einer roten** Tür.

    feminine singular dative
    preceded by indefinite article

*The **old** wine tastes good.*
> ADJECTIVE: **alt** *(old)*
> GENDER: **Der Wein** *(the wine)* is masculine.
> NUMBER: singular
> CASE: nominative
> ARTICLE: definite **der**

Der alte Wein schmeckt gut.
> masculine singular nominative
> preceded by definite article

***Old** wine is expensive.*
> ADJECTIVE: **alt** *(old)*
> GENDER: **Der Wein** *(the wine)* is masculine.
> NUMBER: singular
> CASE: nominative
> ARTICLE: none

Alter Wein ist teuer.
masculine singular nominative
not preceded by article

PREDICATE ADJECTIVES—Predicate adjectives in German have the same form as the dictionary entry for the adjective, regardless of the gender and number of the nouns or pronouns they modify.

*The children are **small**.*
Die Kinder sind **klein**.
>   linking
>   verb
> subject   predicate adjective

*The house is **red**.*
Das Haus ist **rot**.
>   linking
>   verb
> subject   predicate adjective

*I am getting **tired**.*
Ich werde **müde**.
>   linking
>   verb
> subject   predicate adjective

▼▼▼▼▼▼▼▼▼▼▼▼▼▼▼▼REVIEW▼▼▼▼▼▼▼▼▼▼▼▼▼▼▼▼

I. Underline the adjective in the following sentences.
- Draw an arrow from the adjective to the noun or pronoun described.

1. You can't teach an old dog new tricks.

2. This meal is excellent.

3. Which sports are popular in Europe?

II. Underline the predicate adjectives in the following sentences.
- Box in the attributive adjectives. (Remember that in German these attributive adjectives take special endings.)

1. The red onions and green peppers look fresh.

2. New cars have gotten very expensive.

3. The old castle is impressive.

4. Good friends are hard to find.

34. WHAT IS MEANT BY COMPARISON OF ADJECTIVES?

An adjective in its **positive form** refers to the quality of one person or thing.

> My grandfather is *old*.
> This book is *interesting*.

When we speak about two or more nouns that have the same quality, we use **comparison** to indicate that one of these nouns has a greater, lesser, or equal degree of this quality. The adjective that indicates the quality that is being compared changes its form.

<pre>
                    comparison of adjectives
                  ┌───────────────────────┐
     Meg is <i>tall</i> but Todd is <i>taller</i>.
             │   │
     adjective modifying   adjective modifying
     the noun <i>Meg</i>   the noun <i>Todd</i>
</pre>

In both English and German there are two types of comparison: comparative and superlative.

Comparative

IN ENGLISH

Let us go over what is meant by the different types of comparison and how each type is formed.

The **comparative form** compares the quality of one person or thing with the same quality in another person or thing. It can indicate that one or the other has more, less, or the same amount of the quality.

The **comparison of greater degree** (more) is formed by:

- short adjective + *-er* + *than*

> Peter is tall*er than* Anita.
> Beth is calm*er than* her sister.

- *more* + long adjective + *than*

> This book is *more* interesting *than* that one.
> My car is *more* dependable *than* your car.

The **comparison of lesser degree** (less) is formed by:

- *not as* + adjective + *as* or *less* + adjective + *than*

> Meg is *not as* tall *as* Todd.
> Our car is *less* dependable *than* your car.

The **comparison of equal degree** (same) is formed by:

▪ *as* + adjective + *as*

> Jane is *as* tall *as* Mark.
> My car is *as* expensive *as* your car.

IN GERMAN

There are the same types of comparison of adjectives as in English. The comparative of predicate and attributive adjectives is basically formed by adding **-er** to the stem of the adjective. The spelling of some adjectives also changes slightly in the comparative and superlative forms. Your textbook will explain these changes.

▪ a predicate adjective just adds **-er**. This form corresponds to the comparative of many short English adjectives.

> Maria is **jünger** als ihr Bruder.
> jung + -er
> *Maria is **younger** than her brother.*

> Das Buch is **interessanter** als der Film.
> interessant + -er
> *The book is **more interesting** than the film.*

▪ an attributive adjective adds **-er** + the proper adjective ending. Consult your German textbook on how to select the ending.

adjective stem	
jung	Ich kenne das jüng**ere** Mädchen nicht.
	comparative -er + adjective ending **-e**
	*I don't know the **younger** girl.*
interessant	Das ist ein interessant**erer** Film.
	comparative -er + adjective ending **-er**
	*That is a **more interesting** film.*

German also has several irregular comparatives just as English does.

Adjective		Comparative	
gut	*good*	besser	*better*
viel	*much*	mehr	*more*

You will find a list of irregular comparatives in your German textbook which you will have to memorize. Your textbook will also explain how to form the comparisons of lesser degree and of equal degree.

Superlative

IN ENGLISH
The **superlative form** is used to stress the highest or lowest degree of a quality.

The **superlative of highest degree** is formed by:

▪ *the* + short adjective + *-est*

> Mary is *the* calm*est* in the family.
> My car is *the* saf*est* on the market.

▪ *the most* + long adjective

> That argument was *the most* convincing.
> This book is *the most* interesting of all.

The **superlative of lowest degree** is formed by:

▪ *the least* + adjective

> Eric is *the least* tired.
> This radio is *the least* expensive of all.

A few adjectives do not follow this regular pattern of comparison. You must use an entirely different word for the comparative and the superlative.

positive	This apple is *good.*
comparative	This apple is *better.*
	not "gooder"
superlative	This apple is *the best.*
	not "goodest"

IN GERMAN
The superlative degree of the adjective is formed by adding **-st** to the adjective stem (**-est** if the adjective stem ends in **-d, -t, -z, -s,** or **-ß**).

There are small differences in the way the superlative adjective is used depending on whether it is a predicate adjective or an attributive adjective.

▪ a predicate adjective takes the two-word form **am** + adjective + **-st-** (or **-est-**) + **-en**

> Inge ist **am kleinsten.**
> klein + -st- + -en
> *Inge is the smallest.*

Dieses Buch ist **am neuesten**.
neu + -est- + -en
*This book is **the newest**.*

Im Winter ist das Wetter **am kältesten**.
kalt + -est- + -en
In winter the weather is (the) coldest.

- an attributive adjective is preceded by the definitive article (**der, die**, or **das**) and has the appropriate adjective ending that corresponds to the case, number, and gender of the noun it modifies: article + adjective + **-st-** (or **-est-**) + adjective ending.

Inge ist **das kleinste** Mädchen in der Schule.
definite article   klein + -st- + -e
*Inge is **the smallest** girl in the school.*

Die Schallplatten sind alle neu, aber diese ist **die neueste**.
definite article neu + -est- + -e
Schallplatte *(records)* is the unstated, but implied, final word in the sentence modified by **die neueste** *(the newest)*.
*The records are all new, but this is **the newest** one.*

Some superlatives are irregular and will have to be memorized; the same adjectives that are irregular in the comparative are irregular in the superlative.

Positive		Superlative	
gut	*good*	am besten	*best*
viel	*much*	am meisten	*most*

Consult your German textbook for a full list of irregular forms.

▼▼▼▼▼▼▼▼▼▼▼▼▼▼▼▼REVIEW▼▼▼▼▼▼▼▼▼▼▼▼▼▼▼▼

Using the words given, write sentences with comparative adjectives. The various degrees of comparison are indicated as follows:

++ superlative
+ greater degree
= equal degree
- lesser degree

1. The teacher is / (+) old / the students

_____

2. This student is / (=) intelligent / that one.

_____

3. Kathy is / (-) tall / Molly.

_____

4. This movie is / (++) good / this season.

_____

5. Today is / (++) hot / day on record.

_____

35. WHAT IS A POSSESSIVE ADJECTIVE?

A **possessive adjective** is a word that describes a noun by showing who *possesses* that noun. The owner is called the **possessor** and the noun modified is called the person or thing **possessed**.

IN ENGLISH

Here is a list of the possessive adjectives:

Singular

1st person	my
2nd person	your
3rd person	his her its

Plural

1st person	our
2nd person	your
3rd person	their

The possessive adjective refers only to the possessor; it does not agree in gender or number with the object possessed.

Mary's bike is new.
possessor

Her bike is new.
  noun possessed

John's bike is new.
His bike is new.

The cat's ears are short.
Its ears are short.

IN GERMAN

Unlike English, where possessive adjectives refer only to the possessor, German possessive adjectives refer to both the possessor and to the possessed. The possessive adjective itself refers to the person who possesses. The ending on the possessive adjective, however, agrees in case, gender, and number with the noun possessed.

Here are the steps you should follow to choose the proper possessive adjective and to put it in its proper form.

1. POSSESSOR—Indicate the possessor.

	Nominative	
my	mein	
your	dein	(familiar singular)
his	sein	
her	ihr	
its	sein	
our	unser	
your	euer	(familiar plural)
their	ihr	
your	Ihr	(formal)

2. NOUN POSSESSED—Identify and analyze the noun possessed:
   - What is its case?
   - What is its gender?
   - What is its number?

3. ENDING—Provide the ending for the possessive adjective that corresponds to the case, gender, and number of the noun possessed. These endings are the same as those for the indefinite articles, **ein, eine,** and **ein,** as shown in your textbook.

Let us look at some examples:

*He always forgets **his** books.*
   1. POSSESSOR: *his* → **sein**
   2. NOUN POSSESSED: books
      CASE: **Vergessen** *(to forget)* takes a direct object → accusative.
      GENDER: **Das Buch** *(book)* is neuter.
      NUMBER: *Books* is plural.
   3. ENDING: **-e**

Er vergißt immer **seine** Bücher.
            |
      accusative neuter plural

*She gives **her** brother the telephone number.*
   1. POSSESSOR: *her* → **ihr**
   2. NOUN POSSESSED: brother
      CASE: Indirect object of **geben** *(to give)* → dative (She gives
            her number to whom? Her brother.)
      GENDER: **Der Bruder** *(brother)* is masculine.
      NUMBER: *Brother* is singular.
   3. ENDING: **-em**

Sie gibt **ihrem** Bruder die Telefonnummer.
         |
   dative masculine singular

▼▼▼▼▼▼▼▼▼▼▼▼▼▼▼▼REVIEW▼▼▼▼▼▼▼▼▼▼▼▼▼▼▼▼

I. Underline the possessive adjective in the following sentences.
▪ Circle the noun possessed.

1. The students took their exams home.

2. Susan put on her coat and her scarf.

3. Tom put his comb in his pocket.

II. The following examples show you the steps to find the proper form of German possessive adjectives.
▪ Fill in the missing information requested.
▪ Underline the possessive adjective in the German sentence.
▪ Circle the case ending on the German possessive adjective.

1. I am looking for my key.

POSSESSIVE: _____   NOUN POSSESSED: _____

CASE: _____

(**Suchen** *(to look for)* takes a direct object → ending: **-en**)

GENDER: **Der Schlüssel** *(key)* is masculine.

NUMBER: _____

Ich suche **meinen** Schlüssel.

2. We arc helping your aunt.

POSSESSIVE: _____   NOUN POSSESSED: _____

CASE: _____

(**Helfen** *(to help)* takes a dative object → ending: **-er**)

GENDER: **Die Tante** (aunt) is _____

NUMBER: _____

Wir helfen **deiner** Tante.

36. WHAT IS AN INTERROGATIVE ADJECTIVE?

An **interrogative adjective** is a word that asks a question about a noun.

IN ENGLISH
The words *which* and *what* are interrogative adjectives when they come in front of a noun and are used to ask a question. The form of the interrogative adjective never changes regardless of the function of the noun it modifies.

Which book is for sale?
modifies the subject *book*

What courses are you taking?
modifies the direct object *courses*

About *what* film are you talking?
modifies the object of the preposition *about*

IN GERMAN
There is only one interrogative adjective, **welch-**. Here is the singular nominative form for each gender.

masculine	welcher
feminine	welche
neuter	welches

Like all adjectives in German, the interrogative adjective must agree in case, gender, and number with the noun it modifies. The singular nominative form provides the stem to which are added the various endings reflecting the case, gender and number of the noun the interrogative adjective modifies. These endings are the same as for the definite article, **der, die, das**, except in the neuter singular nominative and accusative where the ending **-es** replaces **-as**.

Let us analyze a few examples to see how the interrogative adjective is used in German.

Which *lamp is cheaper?*
    CASE: subject of **sein** *(to be)* → nominative
    GENDER: **Die Lampe** *(lamp)* is feminine.
    NUMBER: singular
Welche Lampe ist billiger?

Which (what) dress do you want to wear?
> CASE: direct object of **tragen** *(to wear)* → accusative
> GENDER: **Das Kleid** *(dress)* is neuter.
> NUMBER: singular

Welches Kleid willst du tragen?

Which man do we give our tickets to?
> CASE: indirect object of **geben** *(to give)* → dative.
>   (**Karten** *(tickets)* is the direct object.)
> GENDER: **Der Mann** *(man)* is masculine.
> NUMBER: singular

Welchem Mann geben wir unsere Karten?

If the noun modified by the interrogative adjective is the object of a preposition, you must begin the question with the preposition followed by the interrogative adjective in the case required by that preposition (see p. 141). Remember to restructure dangling prepositions when expressing an English sentence in German. This will help you identify the object of the preposition and your sentence will correspond to the German sentence structure (see p.143).

Which street does he live on? → *On which street does he live?*
> CASE: object of preposition **in** *(in, on)* → dative
> GENDER: **Die Straße** *(street)* is feminine.
> NUMBER: singular

In welcher Straße wohnt er?

What film are you talking about? → *About what film are you talking?*
> CASE: object of preposition **von** *(about)* → dative
> GENDER: **Der Film** *(film)* is masculine.
> NUMBER: singular

Von welchem Film sprecht ihr?

Careful

The word *what* is not always an interrogative adjective. In the sentence "*What* is on the table?" it is an interrogative pronoun; in German you would ask "**Was** ist auf dem Tisch?" (see **What is an Interrogative Pronoun?**, p. 108).

▼▼▼▼▼▼▼▼▼▼▼▼▼▼▼▼▼▼REVIEW▼▼▼▼▼▼▼▼▼▼▼▼▼▼▼▼▼▼

I. Underline the interrogative adjective in the following sentences.
■ Circle the noun about which a question is being asked.

1. What newspaper do you read?

2. Which record did you buy?

3. Do you know what homework is due?

4. Which hotel are you staying at?

5. Which game did you see?

II. Rewrite these questions in English to eliminate the dangling prepositions.

1. Which topic did you write about?

_____

2. Which people did you talk to?

_____

37. WHAT IS AN ADVERB?

An **adverb** is a word that describes a verb, an adjective, or another adverb.

Kathy drives *well.*
       | |
     verb adverb

The house is *very* big.
           | |
        adverb adjective

The girl ran *too* quickly.
          | |
       adverb adverb

IN ENGLISH
There are different types of adverbs.

- adverbs of manner answer the question *how?* They are the most common adverbs and can usually be recognized by their *-ly* ending.

  They parked the car *carefully.*
  John sang *beautifully.*

- adverbs of quantity or degree answer the question *how much?* or *how well?*

  Mary sleeps *little.*
  This is a *very* cold winter.

- adverbs of time answer the question *when?*

  The children arrived *late.*
  The party started *early.*

- adverbs of place answer the question *where?*

  The old were left *behind.*
  My parents live on the floor *below.*

A few adverbs in English are identical in form to the corresponding adjectives.

Adverb	Adjective
The guests came *late.*	We greeted the *late* guests.
Don't drive so *fast.*	*Fast* drivers cause accidents.
She works very *hard.*	This is *hard* work.

Careful

Remember that in English *good* is an adjective; *well* is an adverb.

That student writes *good* essays.

Good modifies the noun *essays*; it is an adjective.

That student writes *well*.

Well modifies the verb *writes*; it is an adverb.

IN GERMAN

German adverbs have the same form as their corresponding adjectives. They are like the small group of English adverb/adjectives above.

Adverb	Adjective
Wir fahren **schnell**.	Der Wagen ist **schnell**.
We drive fast.	*The car is fast.*
Sie singen **schön**.	Das Lied ist **schön**.
They sing beautifully.	*The song is beautiful.*
Du hast das **gut** gemacht.	Dieses Buch ist **gut**.
You did that well.	*This book is good.*

As in English, there are also words that function only as adverbs.

Das Haus ist **sehr** groß.
The house is very big.

Er kommt **bald**.
He is coming soon.

▼▼▼▼▼▼▼▼▼▼▼▼▼▼▼▼▼▼REVIEW▼▼▼▼▼▼▼▼▼▼▼▼▼▼▼▼▼▼

Circle the adverbs in the sentences below.
- Draw an arrow from each adverb to the word it modifies.

1. The guests arrived early.

2. They were too tired to go out.

3. David learned the lesson really quickly.

4. We stayed here.

5. Meg is a good student who speaks German very well.

38. WHAT IS A PREPOSITION?

A **preposition** is a word that shows the relationship of one word (usually a noun or pronoun) to another word in the sentence. The noun or pronoun which the preposition connects to the rest of the sentence is called the **object of the preposition**. The preposition and its object together make up a **prepositional phrase**.

IN ENGLISH

There are different types of prepositions.

- prepositions showing position

> They are *in* the car.
> She is sitting *behind* you.

- prepositions showing direction

> We went *to* school.
> The students came directly *from* class.

- prepositions showing time

> Many Germans vacation *in* August.
> Their son will be home *at* Christmas.

- prepositions showing manner

> They left *without* us.
> He writes *with* a pen.

IN GERMAN

As in English, prepositions are invariable, i.e., they never change form. However, depending on the preposition, its object can be in the accusative, dative, or genitive case. As you memorize each German preposition, you must memorize the case that follows it.

Below are examples of the various cases that follow prepositions.

> Der Hund läuft **durch die Tür**.
> feminine singular accusative
> **Durch** requires an accusative object.
> *The dog is running **through the door***.

> Er wohnt **bei seiner Tante**.
> feminine singular dative
> **Bei** requires a dative object.
> *He lives **with his aunt***.

Trotz des Regens machten wir einen Spaziergang.

masculine singular genitive
Trotz requires a genitive object.

In spite of the rain we took a walk.

Two-way Prepositions

German also has a group of prepositions called **two-way prepositions**. These prepositions can take either an accusative object or a dative object: an accusative object when they are used with a verb expressing motion in a particular direction, or a dative object when they are used with a verb expressing no directed motion.

Let us look at the prepositions **in** *(into, in)* and **auf** *(on)*:

We are driving into town tomorrow.
Wir fahren morgen **in die Stadt**.

accusative object
to drive implies directed motion

Do you live in the city?
Wohnt ihr **in der Stadt**?

dative object
to live implies no directed motion

He lays the book on the table.
Er legt das Buch **auf den Tisch**.

accusative object
to lay implies directed motion

The book lies on the table.
Das Buch liegt **auf dem Tisch**.

dative object
to lie implies no directed motion

Careful

In learning how to use German prepositions, there are three important things to remember: when to use a preposition, which preposition to use, and where to place it.

USE OF PREPOSITIONS—Every language uses prepositions differently. Do not assume that the same preposition is used in German as in English, or that a preposition will be used in German when you must use one in English (and vice versa).

English	German
preposition →	no preposition
to look *for*	suchen
to look *at*	betrachten
no preposition →	preposition
to answer	antworten **auf**
change of preposition	
to protect *from*	schutzen **vor** *(before)*
to wait *for*	warten **auf** *(on)*
to die *of*	sterben **an** *(at)*

A good dictionary will usually give you the verb plus the preposition when one is required. In particular, be careful not to translate an English verb + preposition word-for-word. For example, when you consult the dictionary to find the German equivalent of *to talk about*, do not stop at the first entry for *talk* (which is **sprechen**) and then add the preposition *about*. Continue searching for the specific meaning *talk about*, which corresponds to the verb **sprechen** with the preposition **über** (which has the primary meanings of *over* or *above*).

> *We **are talking about** politics.*
> Wir **sprechen über** Politik.

On the other hand, when looking up a verb such as **bezahlen** *(to pay for something)*, notice that it is used without a preposition.

> *We **paid for** the meal.*
> Wir **bezahlten** das Essen.

POSITION OF A PREPOSITION—The position of a preposition in an English sentence is much more variable than in a German sentence. Spoken English tends to place the preposition at the end of the sentence, far from its object; this is called a **dangling preposition**. Formal English places the preposition within the sentence or at the beginning of a question. Here are some examples.

Spoken English →	Formal English
Here is the man I talk *with*.	Here is the man *with whom* I talk.
Who(m) are you working *with*?	*With whom* are you working?
That's the teacher I'm talking *about*.	That's the teacher *about whom* I'm talking.

German places prepositions the same way as formal English, that is, within the sentence or at the beginning of a question. Nearly all German prepositions come right before their objects (a few must or can follow their objects); none can be separated from its object. Remember to restructure dangling prepositions when expressing an English sentence in German. This will help you identify the object of the preposition and your sentence will correspond to the German sentence structure. (see p. 143.)

Look at the similarity in the structure of these restructured English sentences and the German sentences that follow.

> *Here is the man I talk* **with**. →
> *Here is the man* **with whom** *I talk.*
> Hier ist der Mann, **mit dem** ich rede.

> *Who are you working* **with**? →
> **With whom** *are you working?*
> **Mit wem** arbeitest du?

> *That is the teacher I am talking* **about**. →
> *That is the teacher* **about whom** *I am talking.*
> Das ist die Lehrerin **von der** ich rede.

Preposition or Prefix?

You will often see German sentences that look as though they end in a preposition:

> Wer kommt **mit**?
> *Who is coming along?*

> Das kommt manchmal **vor**.
> *That happens sometimes.*

> Der Zug hält in München **an**.
> *The train stops in Munich.*

You will easily recognize **mit**, **vor**, and **an** as separable prefixes (see **What are Prefixes and Suffixes?**, p. 146) and not prepositions if you remember that a preposition is never separated from its object. In the sentences above, **mit**, **vor**, and **an** are the separable prefixes of the verbs **mitkommen** *(to come along)*, **vorkommen** *(to happen)*, and **anhalten** *(to stop)*.

▼▼▼▼▼▼▼▼▼▼▼▼▼▼▼▼REVIEW▼▼▼▼▼▼▼▼▼▼▼▼▼▼▼▼▼

I. Circle the prepositions in the following sentences.

1. A mouse darted behind the table.

2. The letter was hidden under the papers.

3. We met at the museum in Stuttgart.

4. On Saturday let's look around the city.

II. Restructure the dangling prepositions in the following sentences so that the structure in English will parallel the structure of a German sentence.

1. I can't tell what they're laughing about.

_____

2. Who are you doing that for?

_____

39. WHAT ARE PREFIXES AND SUFFIXES?

A **prefix** consists of one or more syllables added to the beginning of a word to change that word's meaning.

nuclear   →   *anti*nuclear
believe   →   *dis*believe

A **suffix** consists of one or more syllables added to the end of a word to change that word into a different part of speech.

adjective → **noun**	gentle → gentle*ness*
noun → **adjective**	love → love*able*

To see how prefixes and suffixes work, look at the various English words that come from the Latin verb **duco** *(to lead)*. Different prefixes give us the verbs *in*duce, *re*duce, *se*duce, *pro*duce, *intro*duce, *ad*duce, *e*duce. With suffixes we can produce other different parts of speech, for example: *induction* (noun), *inductive* (adjective), *inductively* (adverb).

IN ENGLISH

Most of our prefixes and suffixes come from Latin and Greek. A good English dictionary will tell you the meanings and functions of the various prefixes and suffixes. Knowing the meaning of prefixes can help you increase your English vocabulary.

anti- + body   →   *anti*body
(against)

sub- + marine   →   *sub*marine
(under)

mal- + nutrition →   *mal*nutrition
(bad)

Likewise, knowing English suffixes can help you identify the parts of speech in a sentence.

-able, -ible	toler*able*	→	**adjective**
-ence, -ance	reli*ance*	→	**noun**
-or	debt*or*	→	**noun**

IN GERMAN

Prefixes and suffixes can communicate even more information than they do in English. Let us look at two of the many ways they affect the nouns and verbs to which they can be attached.

Nouns Formed with Suffixes

Certain suffixes not only affect the meaning of the noun but also determine the gender of the noun.

Suffixes: -chen and **-lein**   **Gender:** The noun will be neuter.

Suffixes showing that the noun is a diminutive, i.e., something reduced in size.

Noun		New Noun	
das Brot	*bread*	das Brötchen	*roll, little bread*
der Brief	*letter*	das Brieflein	*small letter*
die Frau	*woman*	das Fräulein	*young woman, miss*

Suffixes: -heit and **-keit**   **Gender:** The noun will be feminine.

Suffixes which turn an adjective into a noun expressing an abstract quality.

Adjective		New Noun	
schön	*beautiful*	die Schönheit	*beauty*
frei	*free*	die Freiheit	*freedom*
möglich	*possible*	die Möglichkeit	*possibility*

You will find other suffixes used with nouns in the appendix of this book.

Verbs Formed with Prefixes

Verb prefixes are quite versatile and function very differently from English prefixes. They are divided into two groups:

Separable prefixes are prefixes that can be separated from the verb and **inseparable prefixes** are prefixes that cannot be separated from the verb.

We shall consider each type separately.

SEPARABLE PREFIXES—The most common separable prefixes in German are the following.[1]

ab	ein	weiter
an	mit	zu
auf	nach	zurück
aus	vor	

---

[1] Notice that when these units are not prefixes, they function as independent parts of speech. See p. 144.

Let us look at two examples to see how these prefixes can be separated from the verb.

Infinitive	Sentence
ausgehen	Hans und ich **gehen** morgen **aus**.
to go out	present tense
	Hans and I are going out tomorrow.
ankommen	Der Zug **kam** spät **an**.
to arrive	simple past tense
	The train arrived late.

INSEPARABLE PREFIXES—The most common inseparable prefixes in German are the following:

be-	ent-	ge-	zer-
emp-	er-	ver-	

They function more like verb prefixes in English because they are never separated from their stem verb.

Wir **be**suchen unsere Tante.
We're visiting our aunt.

Sie **er**zählte uns eine Geschichte.
She told us a story.

Du **ver**gißt immer dein Buch.
You always forget your book.

When you learn a new verb formed with a prefix, you must memorize whether the prefix is separable or not. You can also learn to recognize the two kinds of verb prefixes by listening to the way they are pronounced.

The separable prefixes are accented (in bold letters):

ankommen
einsteigen
abfahren
mitnehmen

The inseparable prefixes are not accented (accented syllable in bold letters):

be**su**chen
er**fah**ren
ver**lie**ren
zer**fa**llen

Your dictionary will show you which syllable is accented so that you can pronounce the verb correctly.

The addition of a separable or inseparable prefix to a verb has no effect on the conjugation of that verb. The strong and weak verbs include verbs with both types of prefixes (see p. 53). Your German textbook will explain the rules for using verbs with separable and inseparable prefixes in different sentence structures and tenses.

▼▼▼▼▼▼▼▼▼▼▼▼▼▼▼▼▼REVIEW▼▼▼▼▼▼▼▼▼▼▼▼▼▼▼▼▼

I. Underline the prefixes in the following words.

1. decode

2. enlarge

3. misunderstand

II. Underline the suffixes in tthe following words.

1. dependency

2. graceful

3. sleepless

III. Using the Appendix (p. 167) to determine the gender of the nouns based on their suffixes, fill in the appropriate article: **der, die, das.**

1. _____ Vorlesung

2. _____ Journalist

3. _____ Schwierigkeit

4. _____ Mentalität

IV. The bold letters of the following verbs show which syllable is accented. Indicate which verbs have a separable (S) or an inseparable (IS) prefix.

1. **ab**holen	S	IS
2. er**zäh**len	S	IS
3. ge**brau**chen	S	IS
5. **vor**haben	S	IS

40. WHAT IS MEANT BY ACTIVE AND PASSIVE VOICE?

The terms active voice and passive voice are used to describe the relationship between the verb and its subject.

A sentence is in the **active voice** when the subject is the performer of the action.

> The woman reads the novel.
> subject　verb　direct object

> The boy is closing the window.
> subject　verb　direct object

> The medicine healed the patient.
> subject　verb　direct object

In all these examples the subject performs the action of the verb and the direct object receives the action of the verb.

A sentence is in the **passive voice** when the subject is the receiver of the action.

> The novel is read by all literature students.
> subject　verb　agent

> The window is closed by the boy.
> subject　verb　agent

> The patient was healed by the medicine.
> subject　verb　agent

In all these examples the subject receives the action of the verb. The performer of the action, if mentioned, is introduced by the word *by*. The performer is called the **agent**.

Verbs in the passive voice can occur in all the different tenses. The tense of the auxiliary *to be* indicates the tense of the main verb.

> The novel *is read* by the woman.
> present passive

> The novel *was read* by the woman.
> past passive

The novel *has been read* by the woman.

present perfect passive

IN ENGLISH

The passive voice is expressed by the verb *to be* conjugated in the appropriate tense + the past participle of the main verb. In English only transitive verbs (verbs that can have a direct object, see p. 22) can be used in the passive voice.

When an active sentence is changed into a passive one, the following changes occur:

1. The direct object of the active sentence becomes the subject of the passive sentence.

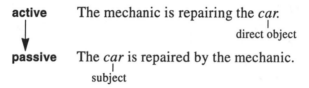

active   The mechanic is repairing the *car.*

direct object

passive   The *car* is repaired by the mechanic.

subject

2. The tense of the verb in the active sentence is reflected in the tense of the verb *to be* in the passive sentence.

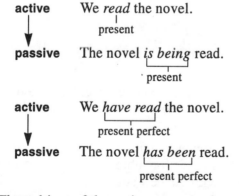

active   We *read* the novel.

present

passive   The novel *is being* read.

· present

active   We *have read* the novel.

present perfect

passive   The novel *has been* read.

present perfect

3. The subject of the active sentence becomes the agent of the passive sentence (although the agent is often omitted).

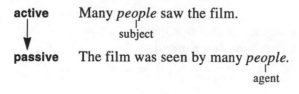

active   Many *people* saw the film.

subject

passive   The film was seen by many *people.*

agent

IN GERMAN

The passive voice is formed by the verb **werden** (literally, *to become)* conjugated in the appropriate tense + the past participle of the main verb.

The tense of passive sentences is indicated by the tense of the verb **werden**; verbs in the passive voice can be in all the different tenses.

> Der Roman **wird** gelesen.
> present
>
> *The novel is (being) read.*

> Der Roman **wurde** gelesen.
> simple past
>
> *The novel was (being) read.*

> Der Roman **wird** gelesen **werden**.
> future
>
> *The novel will be read.*

> Der Roman **ist** gelesen **worden**.
> perfect
>
> *The novel was (has been) read.*

> Der Roman **war** gelesen **worden**.
> pluperfect
>
> *The novel had been read.*

As you can see in the last two examples, **worden**, a contracted form of **geworden** (the past participle of **werden**), is used in the perfect and pluperfect passive.

When you change an active sentence to a passive sentence, you must also remember to use the proper cases for subject and agent and make sure the verb agrees in number with the new subject.

1. The accusative object (AO) of an active sentence becomes the subject (S) of the passive sentence; its case changes from accusative to nominative.

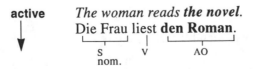

> **active**   *The woman reads **the novel.***
> Die Frau liest **den Roman**.
> S   V   AO
> nom.

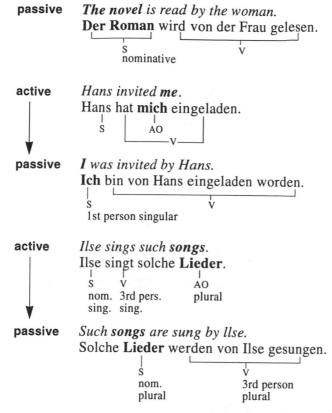

passive   *The novel is read by the woman.*
Der Roman wird von der Frau gelesen.
S
nominative
V

active   *Hans invited me.*
Hans hat **mich** eingeladen.
S   AO
V

passive   *I was invited by Hans.*
Ich bin von Hans eingeladen worden.
S
1st person singular
V

active   *Ilse sings such songs.*
Ilse singt solche **Lieder**.
S   V   AO
nom.   3rd pers.   plural
sing.   sing.

passive   *Such songs are sung by Ilse.*
Solche **Lieder** werden von Ilse gesungen.
S
nom.
plural
V
3rd person
plural

2. If the agent of a passive sentence is a person, it is expressed by **von** + dative object.

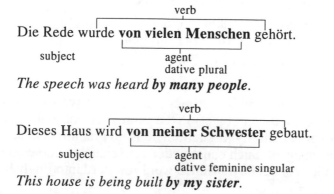

verb
Die Rede wurde **von vielen Menschen** gehört.
subject   agent
dative plural
The speech was heard by many people.

verb
Dieses Haus wird **von meiner Schwester** gebaut.
subject   agent
dative feminine singular
This house is being built by my sister.

3. If the agent is not a person, it is usually expressed by **durch** + accusative object.

Das Gebäude ist **durch das Feuer** zerstört worden.

The building was destroyed by the fire.

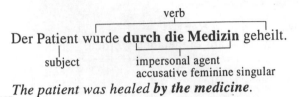

Der Patient wurde **durch die Medizin** geheilt.

The patient was healed by the medicine.

4. If you change a sentence that has only a dative object from active to passive, the dative object does not become the nominative subject of the new sentence. It remains in the dative case. Since these passive sentences have no grammatical subject, the verb is always singular.

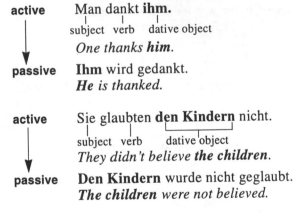

active   Man dankt **ihm.**

One thanks him.

passive   **Ihm** wird gedankt.

He is thanked.

active   Sie glaubten **den Kindern** nicht.

They didn't believe the children.

passive   **Den Kindern** wurde nicht geglaubt.

The children were not believed.

Unlike English, German sometimes uses intransitive verbs (verbs that cannot have a direct object) in the passive voice. In this usage, the verbs express activity as such; there is no grammatical subject and there is no agent. Such constructions are called **impersonal passives**, and they cannot be translated word-for-word into English.

Samstags wird hier getanzt.

adverb   passive verb

There is dancing here on Saturdays.

Jetzt wird hier gearbeitet.

adverb   passive verb

Work is being done here now.

Your textbook will show you several alternatives to the passive construction in German.

▼▼▼▼▼▼▼▼▼▼▼▼▼▼▼▼▼REVIEW▼▼▼▼▼▼▼▼▼▼▼▼▼▼▼▼▼

I. Underline the subject in the following sentences.
- Circle the performer of the action.
- Identify each sentence as active (A) or passive (P).

1. The cow jumped over the moon.   A   P

2. The game was cut short by rain.   A   P

3. They camped by the river.   A   P

4. We were awakened by a loud noise.   A   P

5. This film will be enjoyed by everyone.   A   P

II. Underline the verb in the following sentences..
- Identify the tense of each sentences: past (PA), present (P), future (F).
- Keeping the same tense, rewrite the sentence in the passive voice on the line provided.

1. The parents dropped off the children.   PA   P   F

_____

2. Work crews are clearing the road.   PA   P   F

_____

3. People all over the world will see this program.   PA   P   F

_____

41. WHAT IS A CONJUNCTION?

A **conjunction** is a word that links words or groups of words.

IN ENGLISH
There are two kinds of conjunctions: coordinating and subordinating.

Coordinating conjunctions join words, phrases, and clauses that are equal; they coordinate elements of equal rank. The major coordinating conjunctions in English are *and, but, or, nor,* and *for.*

> good *or* evil
> over the river *and* through the woods
> They invited us, *but* we couldn't come.

Subordinating conjunctions join a dependent clause to the main clause; they subordinate one thought to another one; that is, they indicate the relationship of unequal elements. A clause introduced by a subordinating conjunction is called a **dependent** or **subordinate clause** (see p. 163). Typical subordinating conjunctions are *although, because, if, unless, so that, while, that,* and *whatever.*

> *Although* we were invited, we didn't go.
> subordinating conjunction   main clause

> They left *because* they were bored.
> main clause   subordinating conjunction

> He said *that* he was tired.
> main clause subordinating conjunction

Note that the main clause is not always the first clause of the sentence.

Preposition or Subordinating Conjunction?

Some words function as both prepositions and subordinating conjunctions. We can decide which one by determining whether or not the word in question introduces a clause.

If the word in question introduces a clause, it is a subordinating conjunction. The clause will contain a subject and a verb (see **What are Sentences, Phrases, and Clauses?**, p. 159).

We left *before* the intermission began.

        subordinating   subject + verb
        conjunction

After the concert was over, we ate ice cream.

    subordinating subject + verb
    conjunction

If the word in question does not introduce a clause, it is a preposition. The prepositional phrase contains an object, but no verb.

We left *before* the intermission.

      preposition   object of preposition

After the concert we ate ice cream.

  preposition object of preposition

IN GERMAN

Memorize conjunctions as vocabulary items. Like adverbs and prepositions, conjunctions are invariable (i.e., they never change their form), but they do have their own rules of usage. Your German textbook will explain these special rules.

The major coordinating conjunctions are **und** *(and)*, **oder** *(or)*, **aber** *(but)*, **sondern** *(but, on the contrary)*, and **denn** *(for)*. Typical subordinating conjunctions include **obgleich** *(although)*, **obwohl** *(although)*, **weil** *(because)*, **wenn** *(if, whenever)*, **damit** *(in order that)*, **daß** *(that)*, and **während** *(while)*.

Careful

It is important for you to establish whether a word is a preposition or a conjunction, because in German you will use different words and apply different rules of grammar depending on the part of speech. In English it is easy to overlook the part of speech to which a word belongs because we sometimes use the same word as a preposition and as a conjunction.

ENGLISH preposition and conjunction	GERMAN preposition	conjunction
before	vor	bevor
after	nach	nachdem

Let us look at some examples using these different parts of speech.

> *We left **before** the intermission.*
>   preposition   object of preposition
> Wir sind **vor** der Pause weggegangen.

> *We left **before** the intermission began.*
>   subordinating   subject + verb
>   conjunction
> Wir sind weggegangen, **bevor** die Pause anfing.

> ***After** the concert we ate ice cream.*
> preposition   object of preposition
> **Nach** dem Konzert haben wir Eis gegessen.

> ***After** the concert was over, we ate ice cream.*
> subordinating   subject + verb
> conjunction
> **Nachdem** das Konzert vorbei war, aßen wir Eis.

Make sure that you know the part of speech of the new words that you learn, so that you can use the proper word in German and apply the proper rules of grammar.

▼▼▼▼▼▼▼▼▼▼▼▼▼▼▼REVIEW▼▼▼▼▼▼▼▼▼▼▼▼▼▼▼

I. Circle the coordinating and subordinating conjunctions.
■ Underline the words each conjunction serves to coordinate or to subordinate.

1. We can have a picnic unless it starts raining.

2. She stopped studying because she was too tired.

3. He forgot his watch, but he remembered his passport.

II. Underline the prepositions in the following sentences.
■ Box in the conjunctions.

1. Since the weather turned cold, we'll stayed inside.

2. I've know him since high school.

3. We were home before midnight.

4. Before we leave, we'd better say goodbye.

42. WHAT ARE SENTENCES, PHRASES, AND CLAUSES?

When you speak or write in English or in German, you use sentences, phrases, and clauses to express your thoughts.

What is a Sentence?

A **sentence** is a group of words that act together as a complete unit. Typically a sentence consists of at least a subject (see **What is a Subject?**, p. 24) and a verb (see **What is a Verb?**, p. 21).

> We ran.
> subject verb

> They were eating.
> subject   verb

> Where are you going?
> adverb   subject
>   — verb —

Depending on the verb, a sentence may also have direct and indirect objects (see **What are Objects?**, p. 26).

> She threw the ball.
> subject verb   direct object

> They gave him a present.
> subject verb indirect   direct
>   object   object

In addition, a sentence may include various kinds of modifiers: adjectives (see **What is an Adjective?**, p. 123), adverbs (see **What is an Adverb?**, p. 139), prepositional phrases (see **What is a Preposition?**, p. 141), and participial phrases (see **What is a Participle?**, p. 71).

> I saw a movie.
>   verb   object
> subject

> I saw a *great* movie.
>   adjective

> *Yesterday* I saw a great movie.
> adverb

Yesterday *after work* I saw a great movie.

prepositional phrase modifying *saw*

Attracted by the reviews, I saw a great movie yesterday.

participial phrase modifying *I*

Although not all these elements occur in a German sentence in the same way that they do in English, you will find it very helpful to recognize the different parts of a sentence in each language. Moreover, it will be important for you to recognize complete sentences and to distinguish phrases and clauses from complete sentences.

What is a Phrase?

A **phrase** is simply a group of words that belong together on the basis of their meaning. We identify phrases by the type of word that introduces them.

A **prepositional phrase** begins with a preposition.

through the door

preposition   object of preposition

after the concert

preposition   object of preposition

A **participial phrase** begins with a participle.

leaving the room

present participle   object of *leaving*
of *to leave*

pasted on the wall

past participle   prepositional phrase used
of *to paste*   adverbially to modify *pasted*

A **infinitive phrase** begins with an infinitive.

to learn German

infinitive   object of *to learn*

to read intelligently

infinitive   adverb modifying *to read*

To recognize such phrases you need to find the individual parts (prepositions, participles, infinitives) and determine how the group of words works as one block of meaning.

What is a Clause?

A **clause** is a group of words that contains its own subject and conjugated verb.

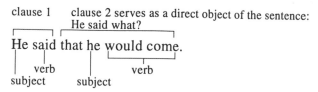

You can distinguish these clauses from a phrase by the presence of a subject and a conjugated verb in each one (see p. 57). You can see that they are different from a complete sentence if you try to use them separately. Neither "he said" nor "that he would come" expresses a finished thought; therefore neither is a complete sentence. Instead, both are parts of a whole sentence.

Simple Sentences

A **simple sentence** is a sentence consisting of only one clause.

IN ENGLISH

There is no set position for the verb in an English sentence or clause, but the subject almost always comes before the verb.

We went to the concert.
| |
subject verb

A modifier can also come before the subject.

Yesterday we went to a concert.
|
adverb

After the party we went to a concert.
|
prepositional phrase modifying *went*

IN GERMAN

In a simple declarative sentence (a statement), the conjugated verb always stands in second position. This does not mean that the verb is always the second word in the sentence; it means that if the sentence begins with some modifier, for example, an adverb or a prepositional phrase, the verb follows immediately. Compare the structure of these German sentences with that of their literal English translation.

> Wir **gingen** in ein Konzert.
> *we* ***went*** *to a concert*
> | |
> subject verb
> 1 2

> Gestern **gingen** wir in ein Konzert.
> *yesterday* ***went*** *we to a concert*
> | | |
> adverb verb subject
> 1 2

> Nach der Party **gingen** wir in ein Konzert.
> *after the party* ***went*** *we to a concert*
> └─────────┘ | |
> prepositional verb subject
> phrase 2
> 1

> Gestern abend nach der Party **gingen** wir in ein Konzert.
> *yesterday evening after the party* ***went*** *we to a concert*
> | └───────────┘ | |
> adverb prepositional verb subject
> | phrase modifying 2
> | **gestern abend**
> └──────────┘
> adverbial modifiers
> functioning as
> a single unit of meaning
> 1

Only in the first example is it possible to put the subject before the verb in the German sentence. In the other sentences that space is already occupied by a modifier; the verb must come second, and the subject must follow the verb.

Compound Sentences

A **compound sentence** consists of two equal clauses joined by a coordinating conjunction (see **What is a Conjunction?**, p. 156). In both English and German the word order is the same as for any simple sentence.

IN ENGLISH

The position of the verb can vary in a simple sentence, though the subject usually comes before the verb.

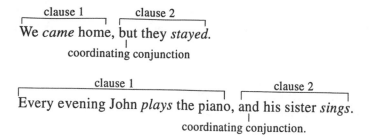

IN GERMAN

It is important that you know how to recognize a compound sentence. Usually the two statements of a compound sentence are both simple sentences. This means that in German each statement will have the conjugated verb in second position:

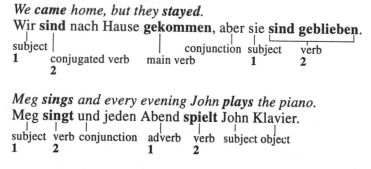

The coordinating conjunction between the two clauses has no effect on the word order of the second clause.

Complex Sentences

A **complex sentence** is a sentence consisting of a main clause and one or more dependent clauses.

The **main clause** (or **independent clause**) in a complex sentence could stand alone as a complete sentence.

The **dependent clause** (including relative clauses) cannot stand alone as a complete sentence; it depends on the main clause for its full meaning, and it is subordinate to the main clause.

dependent clause   main clause
Although it was raining, we took a walk.

It makes sense to say "we took a walk" without the first clause in the sentence; therefore, it is the main clause. It does not make sense to say, "although it was raining" unless we add a conclusion; therefore, it is the dependent clause.

IN ENGLISH
Distinguishing a main clause from a dependent clause helps you to write complete sentences and avoid sentence fragments.

IN GERMAN
It is important for you to learn to distinguish between the main clause and the dependent clause in German, because each type of clause has its own word order.

In the main clause the verb remains in the same position as in the simple sentence; that is, the verb will be in second position in a German sentence, unlike in English where the position may vary.

*Although it was raining, we **took** a walk.*
dependent clause   subject verb
functions as a single   2   3
unit of meaning
1

Obwohl es regnete, **machten** wir einen Spaziergang.
dependent clause   verb   subject
functions as a single   2   3
unit of meaning
1

In dependent clauses (clauses introduced by subordinating conjunctions and relative pronouns), the conjugated verb stands at the end, except in a few special constructions.

*Although it **was** beginning to rain, we took a walk.*
          conjugated
   subject verb
subordinating
conjunction

Obwohl es zu regnen **anfing**, machten wir einen Spaziergang.
   subject   conjugated
subordinating   verb
conjunction

Your German textbook will explain this structure in more detail.

▼▼▼▼▼▼▼▼▼▼▼▼▼▼▼REVIEW▼▼▼▼▼▼▼▼▼▼▼▼▼▼▼▼▼

I. Underline the phrases in these sentences.

1. It is important to do your best.

2. Before the play we ate out.

3. Chris remembered the appointment at the last minute.

4. They wanted to start early in the morning.

5. Jane spent an hour organizing her room.

II. Box in the dependent clauses in these sentences.

1. While you were out, someone called.

2. Although we were tired, we had fun.

3. They said that they were ready.

4. Let us know if you want to go with us.

5. After the sun set, the park closed for the day.

III. Underline the verb in the main clause.
▪ Write "2" above this verb to indicate that it would be in second position in a German sentence.

1. Last night it snowed.

2. They really looked surprised.

3. With computers the work goes faster.

4. Tomorrow I have an appointment.

5. By the time we arrived, things were over.

Appendix
Selected Noun Gender Reference List

1. MASCULINE (**maskulin**)

- Nouns referring to masculine persons which end in **-er, -ist, -ling, -ent**. Plural formed by adding **—, -e,** or **-en.**

der Physiker	die Physiker
der Jüngling	die Jünglinge
der Pianist	die Pianisten
der Referent	die Referenten

A more general rule: nouns referring to human beings are masculine unless they specifically refer to females (which then have feminine gender). Be careful, however, with diminutives (das Fräulein, das Mädchen), which are discussed below.

- Names of seasons, months, days, parts of days (except **die Nacht**), geographical directions, and weather phenomenona.

der Sommer
der Januar
der Montag
der Mittag
der Wind
der West

Note: **das Frühjahr,** another terms for **der Frühling,** is neuter because **Jahr** is neuter.

- Most nouns which end in:

-ig	der Pfennig
-or	der Motor, der Doktor
-ismus	der Optimismus

2. FEMININE (**feminin**)

- Most 2-syllable nouns which end in **-e**. Plural formed by adding **-n.**

die Lampe	die Lampen
die Seife	die Seifen

(Some common exceptions are: **der Name, der Käse, das Auge.**)

- Nouns referring to female human beings which end in **-in**. Plural formed by adding **-nen.**

die Studentin	die Studentinnen
die Professorin	die Professorinnen

- Nouns which end in:

-ei	die Bücherei	die Büchereien
-ie	die Drogerie	die Drogerien
-heit	die Dummheit	die Dummheiten
-keit	die Möglichkeit	die Möglichkeiten
-schaft	die Mannschaft	die Mannschaften
-ung	die Prüfung	die Prüfungen
-ion	die Reaktion	die Reaktionen
-tät	die Universität	die Universitäten
-ade	die Fassade	die Fassaden
-ik	die Musik	
-ur	die Natur	
-unft	die Vernunft	
-enz	die Lizenz	die Lizenzen

3. NEUTER (neutral)

- Nouns ending in the diminutives suffixes **-lein** or **-chen**. Plural just like singular.

das Mädchen	die Mädchen
das Büchlein	die Büchlein
das Fräulein	die Fräulein

- Verb infinitives used as nouns (gerunds). No plural possible.

  das Lesen
  das Essen
  das Singen

- The names of most cities, continents, and countries.

  (das) Berlin
  (das) Europa
  (das) Deutschland

Note: Unless preceded by an adjective, articles are not usually used with these nouns. There are important exceptions as well, masculine and feminine place names that do take articles, for example:

  die Antarktis
  die Bundesrepublik Deutschland
  der Libanon
  die Schweiz

- Most nouns which end in **-um**. Plural with ¨er.

  das Bistum   die Bistümer

ANSWER KEY

1. What is a Noun? 1. student, teacher, question 2. textbook, picture, cover 3. Eric, tape deck, birthday 4. cows, middle, field 5. actions, words 6. audience, wit, candor

2. What is Meant by Gender? I. 1. ? 2. F 3. M 4. ? 5. ? II. 1. M 2. N 3. F 4. M 5. F

3. What is Meant by Number? I. 1. plural 2. singular 3. singular 4. plural 5. singular II. 1. ö + -er 2. ü + -e 3. -er 4. -en 5. -s

4. What are Articles? I. 1. **das** 2. **die** 3. **der** 4. **die** 5. **das** II. 1. the 2. a 3. the 4. a 5. the

5. What is Meant by Case? I. 1. the children, the ball 2. the cat, the mice 3. a car, the drive 4. an insider, the story, the press 5. the end, the movie, a surprise

6. What is a Verb? 1. eat 2. met 3. stayed, expected 4. took, finished, went 5. felt, talked

7. What is a Subject? 1. Q:What leaves? A:The bus. 2. Q: What was over? A: The game. Q: Who went home? A: Everyone. 3. Q: Who took a boat ride? A: My friends and I.

8. What are Objects? 1. Q: What did the computer lose? A: My homework. DO 2. Q: What did she send? A: A postcard. Q:To whom did she send it? A: To her friend. DO + IO 3. Q: For what did they pay? A: The books. Q: With what did they pay? A: A credit card. OP + OP

9. What is a Predicate Noun? The subject is between parentheses: 1. news (letter) 2. doctor (Carol) 3. tourists (they) 4. musician (Dan) 5. place (pool)

10. What is the Possessive? The possessor is in *italics*: 1. the motor of the *car* 2. the results of a *test* 3. the end of the *year* 4. the tale of two *cities* 5. the works of *Bachmann*

11. What is a Pronoun? The antecedent is between parentheses: 1. she (Brooke) 2. they (Molly and Stan) 3. it (chair) 4. himself (Jim) 5. her (Helga)

12. What is a Personal Pronoun? I. 1. **du** 2. **wir** 3. **ihr** 4. **Sie** II. 1. it, **es** 2. it, **sie** 3. it, **er** III. Nouns referring to persons are in *italics*: 1. *Greg*, preposition + pronoun 2. present, **da**-compound

3. *Emily*, preposition + pronoun 4. vacation, **da**-compound
IV. 1. 2nd person, singular, dative 2. 3rd person, masculine, singular, accusative

13. What are the Principal Parts of a Verb? 1. W 2. S
3. S 4. W 5. S

14. What is an Infinitive? 1. teach 2. be 3. have 4. leave 5. swim

15. What is a Verb Conjugation? I. 1. **denk-** 2. **renn-** 3. **arbeit-**
4. **wander-** 5. **reis-** II. STEM: **geh-**; gehe, gehst, geht, gehen, geht,
gehen

17. What is the Present Tense? 1. do play, **spielen** 2. plays, **spielt**
3. is playing, **spielt** 4. are playing, **spielen** 5. do play, **spielst**

18. What is the Past Tense? I. 1. wrote, was writing, did write
2. laughed, was laughing, did laugh II. 1. spoke 2. rained 3. telephoned

19. What are Auxiliary Verbs? I. 1. are 2. can 3. do 4. has been
5. will II. English auxiliary verbs that will not be expressed by
auxiliary verbs in German are in parenthese: 1. (is) coming 2.
reads 3. drives 4. (are) packing 5. (does) have

20. What is a Participle? I. 1. working; present 2. spilled; past
3. falling; present 4. sunken; past 5. heated; past II. Participles are
in *italics*: 1. *coming* 2. littering 3. sunbathing 4. *turning*

21. What are the Perfect Tenses? 1. had said (-2), climbed (-1)
2. wants (0), called (-1)

22. What is the Future Tense? 1. are going → present 2. is → future
of probability 3. shall return → future 4. will tell →future 5. '11
be →future 6. cost →future of probability

23. What is Meant by Mood? 1. indicative 2. subjunctive 3. imperative 4. indicative 5. imperative

24. What is the Imperative? 1. **du** 2. **wir** 3. **ihr** 4. Sie 5. **du**

25. What is the Subjunctive? I. 1. F 2. CTF 3. CTF 4. F 5. CTF
II. 1. were → P 2. would do → P; had → P 3. had planned → PA;
would have packed → PA 4. would like → P 5. were → P; would
wear → P 6. had called → PA; would have come → PA 7. had
stopped → PA

26. What is Meant by Direct and Indirect Discourse? 1. is →present, how the weather was 2. found →past, we, they had found the
trail 3. got → past, I/my, he had just gotten his driver's license 4.
'm coming →present, I, ... she was coming 5. 'm done →present, I,

... he was done

27. What is a Possessive Pronoun? 1. yours 2. ours 3. hers 4. his
5. mine

28. What is a Reflexive Pronoun? 1. yourself 2. ourselves 3. himself 4. herself 5. myself 6. yourselves

28. What is a Reflexive Verb? **mich, dich, sich, uns, euch, sich**

29. What is an Interrogative Pronoun? 1. who, person, subject →
wer 2. what, thing, direct object → **was** 3. whose, person (or
thing), possessive → **wessen** 4. who (for whom), person, object of
preposition → **wen**

30. What is a Relative Pronoun? The antecedent is in *italics*: I.
1. that, *letter,* DO 2. who, *people,* S 3. whom, *woman*, DO
4. whose, *book*, PM 5. whom, *student*, OP II. 1. dog/it, *dog*, it,
subject, that (which) → The dog that lives next door is friendly.
2. Smiths/them, *Smiths,* them, direct object, who(m) → The Smiths,
who(m) you met in Basel, left for Austria. 3. student/her, *student*,
her, object of preposition, who(m) → The new student, about whom
you were asking, is German./The new student you were asking
about is German.

32. What is a Descriptive Adjective? I. The noun or pronoun
described is between parentheses: 1. old (dog); new (tricks)
2. excellent (meal) 3. popular (sports) II. Predicate adjectives are
in *italics:* 1. *fresh;* red, green 2. *expensive;* new 3. *impressive;* old
4. *hard to find;* good

33. What is Meant by Comparison of Adjectives? 1. The teacher is
older than the students. 2. This student is as intelligent as that one.
3. Kathy is less tall than Molly. 4. This movie is the best this
season. 5. Today is the hottest day on record.

34. What is a Possessive Adjective? I. The possessive adjective is in
italics: 1. *their* exams 2. *her* coat, *her* scarf 3. *his* comb, *his* pocket
II. 1. my, key, singular, accusative, **mein + -en** 2. your, aunt, feminine, singular, **dein + -er**

35. What is an Interrogative Adjective? I. The interrogative adjective is in *italics:* 1. *what* newspaper 2. *which* record 3. *what* homework 4. *which* hotel 5.*which* game II. 1. About which topic did
you write? 2. To which people did you talk?

36. What is an Adverb? The word modified is after the comma: 1.
early, arrived 2. too, tired 3. really, quickly, learned 4. here, stayed
5. very, well, speaks

37. What is a Preposition? I. 1. behind 2. under 3. at, in 4. on, around II. 1. I can't tell about what they're laughing. 2. For whom are you doing that?

38. What are Prefixes and Suffixes? I. 1. **de-** 2. **en-** 3. **mis-** II. 1. -ency 2. -ful 3. -less III. 1. **die** 2. **der** 3. **die** 4. **die** IV. 1. S 2. IS 3. IS 4. S

39. What is Meant by Active and Passive Voice? I. The performer of the action is in *italics:* 1. cow, *cow* → A 2. game, *rain* → P 3. they, *they* → A 4. we, *noise* → P 5. film, everyone → P II. 1. dropped, past → The children were dropped off by the parents. 2. are clearing, present → The road is being cleared by work crews. 3. will see, future → This program will be seen by people all over the world.

40. What is a Conjunction? I. The conjunctions are in *italics*: 1. *unless,* it starts raining 2. *because,* she was too tired 3. *but,* he remembered his passport II. The conjunctions are in *italics*: 1. *since* 2. since 3. before 4. *before*

41. What are Sentences, Phrases, and Clauses? I. 1. *to do your best* 2. *Before the play* 3. *at the last minute* 4. *to start early, in the morning* 5. *organizing her room* II. 1. While you were out 2. Although we were tired 3. that they were ready 4. if you want to go with us 5. After the sun set III. 1. snowed 2. looked 3. goes 4. have 5. were

INDEX

a, an 12-3
  see also indefinite article
accusative 18-9, 27, 30, 44-9, 152-3
  object of preposition 30, 141-2, 154
  of interrogative pronoun 109-11
  of personal pronoun 45
  of reflexive pronoun 104
  with preposition 30-1
active voice 150-5
adjective 71-3, 123, 124-7
  attributive 71-3, 75, 77, 124-6,
  129, 131
  comparative 128-31
  demonstrative 123
  descriptive 123, 124-7
  interrogative 123, 136-7
  possessive 101, 123, 133-4
  predicate 124, 126-7
adjective endings 125-6
  strong 125
  weak 125
adverb 80, 83-4, 139-40
agent 150
  impersonal 154
  in passive voice 150-5
  personal agent 153
agreement 11, 25, 39, 83, 97, 102,
  133-4, 152
antecedent 38-9, 46-9, 114
  indefinite 120
  of personal pronoun 42-3, 46-9
  of relative pronoun 114-21
apostrophe 34-5
article 11-3
  see also definite article *and*
  indefinite article
attributive adjective 71-3, 75, 77,
  124-6, 129, 131
  in comparative degree 128-30
  in superlative degree 130-1
auxiliary verb 63, 67-70, 79-80, 150

be 67, 69
  in passive voice 151
  in subjunctive 91, 92

case 13, 15-20, 24, 27, 123, 125,
  133-4, 136, 152
  of interrogative pronoun 109-12
  of personal pronoun 40-1, 43-50
  of reflexive pronon 103-5, 107
  of relative pronoun 117-8
class 2
clause 161
  dependent 114, 163-4
  relative 114
  subordinate 114, 156-7
cognate 1
collective noun 9
command 88-9
common noun 4
compound noun 4
compound tense 65, 71, 79
conditional 91, 95
conjugated verb 25, 55, 57-61, 162-4
conjugation 23, 57-61
conjunction 156-8
  co-ordinating 156-7
  subordinating 156-7
contrary-to-fact condition 90-1, 93-4

da-compound 50
dative 18-9, 27-30, 44-5
  in passive sentence 154
  object of verb 27-8
  of interrogative pronoun 110-1
  of personal pronoun 45
  of reflexive pronoun 104-5
  with preposition 30, 36, 141-2, 153
declension 11-3, 17-20, 117-8,
  125, 136
demonstrative adjective 123
descriptive adjective 123, 124-7
direct discourse 97-8

direct object
　see object, direct
do, does 67-8

extended adjectival construction 72-3, 77

familiar you 41-2, 45-6, 59
feminine 6-7, 12-3, 36, 43, 46-7, 147
finite verb 55
first person 40-1, 57-9, 97
formal you 41-2, 45-6, 59
function 2-3, 11, 15, 18-20, 40, 45-8, 109-12, 117-20
future of probability 84
future perfect tense 52, 80-2
future tense 52, 62, 67-8, 83-4

ge- prefix 53,76
gender 6-7, 18, 39, 42-3, 46-8, 100, 125-7, 133, 136, 167-8
genitive 19, 35-6, 41, 141-2
gerund 73-4, 168

haben 67, 77, 80-2, 93, 98
have 67, 75, 79-80
he 38, 40-1, 44
helping verb 67-70
　see also **haben, sein, werden**
her 2, 17, 44-5, 48, 133-4
hers 100
herself 39, 102, 104
him 44-5, 48
himself 102, 104
his 100, 133-4

I 16, 38, 40-1, 44, 57-8
idiom 2
if-clause 91, 93-4
imperative 88-9
imperfect tense
　see simple past
impersonal passive 154
indefinite antecedents 120
indefinite articles 12-3, 17, 125
indicative 86, 88, 91-3
indirect discourse subjunctive 97-8

indirect object
　see object, indirect
infinitive 52-4, 55-6, 70, 83, 92, 95, 106, 148, 160
-ing 71, 73
　gerund 73-4
　participle 71-2
inseparable prefix 148-9
interrogative adjective 123, 136-7
interrogative pronoun 39, 108-12, 137
intransitive verb 22, 154
irregular verb 53, 75
it 38, 40-7, 49-50
its 100, 133-4
itself 102, 104

let's 88
linking verb 32-3, 124
-ly ending of adverb 139

main clause 163-4
main verb 55, 67-9, 79-80, 83
masculine 6-7, 12-3, 35, 43, 46-8
me 16, 38, 40, 44-5
meaning 1
mine 39, 100-1
modal auxiliary 69-70
mood 86
　imperative 86, 88
　in indirect discourse 97
　indicative 86
　subjunctive 86, 90-5
my 133-4
myself 39, 102-5

necessity, expression of 90
neuter 6-7, 12-3, 35, 42-3, 45-7, 147
nominative 16, 18-9, 24, 32-3, 152
　of interrogative pronoun 108-10
　of personal pronoun 40-4
non-restrictive clause 121
noun 4-5, 39, 42, 146-7, 167-8
　agreement with article 11
　collective 9
　used as adjective 4-5
　verbal noun 73-4, 168
number 9-10, 39, 110, 125-6, 133, 136

object 22, 26-31, 43-50, 102-5, 108-11, 115-8
  direct 16, 22, 26-7, 29, 44, 102-4, 110, 115
  indirect 16, 26, 28-9, 44, 103-4, 110-1, 115
  of preposition 16, 26, 29-31, 44, 48-50, 74, 103-5, 109-10, 115-6
objective 16-7, 44
of 34, 36
our 133-4
ours 100
ourselves 102, 104

part of speech 2-3, 146
participial phrase 72, 75, 160
participle 69,71-7, 160
  past 52-4, 75-7, 98, 152
  present 69, 71-4
passive voice 67-8, 77, 150-5
past emphatic 65
past participle 52-4, 75-7, 98, 152
past perfect 52, 65, 79-81
  see also pluperfect
past progressive 65
past subjunctive 93-4
past tense 52-4, 62, 65
  past emphatic 65
  past progressive 65
  simple past 52, 65, 91
perfect tense 65, 67, 79-82, 152
personal endings 60
personal pronoun 38, 40-50, 103
  in imperative 88-9
  as object 38, 43-8
  as object of preposition 38, 48-50
  as subject 38, 40-3
phrase 159-61
  participial 72, 75, 160
  prepositional 141, 160
  infinitive 160
pluperfect 79-81, 152
plural 9-10, 34, 40-2, 58-60, 167-8
Plusquamperfekt
  see pluperfect
possessive 17, 34-6, 108, 112, 116
possessive adjective 101, 123, 133-4

possessive pronoun 17, 39, 100-1
predicate adjective 124-7
predicate noun 16, 19, 32-3
prefix 53, 76, 144, 146-9
  inseparable 148-9
  separable 144, 147-8
preposition 29-31, 141-4, 156-8
  dangling 111, 116, 137, 143-4
  object of
    see object of preposition
  two-way 142
prepositional phrase 141, 160
present participle 69, 71-7, 160
present perfect 65, 79
present subjunctive 90-3
present tense 52, 57-61, 62, 63, 83-4, 89
  emphatic 63
  perfect 79-81
  progressive 63
preterite tense
  see simple past
principal parts 52-4
pronominal adverb 50
pronoun 15-7, 38-9, 40-50, 97
  direct object 38, 44-8
  indirect object 38, 44-8
  interrogative 39, 108-12
  object 16, 38, 43-8
  object of preposition 16, 38, 48-50, 105, 108, 115-8
  possessive 17, 39
  reflexive 39, 102-5
  relative 39, 114-21
  subject 16, 38, 40-3, 57-60, 88-9, 102
proper noun 4, 34-6

reflexive pronoun 39, 102-5
reflexive verb 106-7
regular verb 52, 75
relative clause 114-21, 164
relative pronoun 39, 114-21
requests 94
restrictive clause 121

second-person 40-2, 44-6, 54, 57-9
sein 67, 77, 80-2, 93, 98
sentence 26, 159-60
   complete 21
   complex 163-4
   compound 162-3
   simple 161-2
separable prefix 144, 147-8
shall 83
she 38, 40-1, 43-4
simple past 52, 62, 65, 91-2
simple tense 65
singular 9-10, 40-1, 44-5
some 13
statement 162
stem of verb 60, 76, 92, 98
strong verbs 53, 61, 65, 76, 149
subject 16, 19, 24-5, 32-3, 38-9, 40-3,
   57-60, 102-4, 106-7, 114, 117-8,
   150-2, 154, 159
subjunctive 86, 90-5
   general subjunctive 92-4, 98
   special subjunctive 97-8
   subjunctive I 97
   subjunctive II 92-4, 97
subordinate clause 114, 156-7, 163
suffix 76, 146-7, 167-8

tense 62
that 2, 115
the 11-2, 18
   see also definite article
their 133-4
theirs 100
them 16-7, 40, 44-5
themselves 102-4
they 16, 40-1, 44, 59, 102
third person 40-8, 53-4, 57-60

umlaut 10
us 16, 38, 43-5
use 2

verb 21-3, 52-4, 55-6, 57-61, 62,
67-70, 71-7
   auxiliary 63, 67-70, 79-80, 150
   intransitive 22, 154

irregular 53-75
reflexive 106-7
regular 52, 75
transitive 22, 151
strong 53, 61, 65, 76, 149
weak 53, 65, 76, 149
with prefixes 147-9
verbal noun 73-4
vocabulary 1
voice 150-5

we 16, 40-1, 44, 59
   command 88-9
weak verbs 53, 65, 76, 149
werden 67-8, 77, 83-4, 95, 152
what 39
   interrogative adjective 136-7
   interrogative pronoun 39, 109,
   112, 137
which 115-6, 136-7
   relative pronoun 115-6
   interrogative pronoun 136-7
who 39, 108-10, 114, 116
   interrogative pronoun 39, 108-10
   relative pronoun 39, 114, 116
whom 39, 108-11, 115-6
   interrogative pronoun 108-11
   relative pronoun 115-6
whose 39, 108, 112, 116
   interrogative pronoun 108, 112
   relative pronoun 116
will 83
wishes 90-1, 94
word order 15-7, 83, 143-4, 162-4
would 93, 95
would have 94
würde-construction 95

you 40-2, 44-6, 57-9
   command 88-9
   familiar 42, 45-6, 58-9
   formal 42, 46, 59
your 133-4
yours 39, 100
yourself 102, 104-5
yourselves 102, 104